THE RENAISSANCE
IN THE FIELDS

DUCCIO BALESTRACCI

THE RENAISSANCE
IN THE FIELDS

Family Memoirs
of a
Fifteenth-Century Tuscan Peasant

Translated by
Paolo Squatriti and Betsy Merideth

With an Introduction by
Edward Muir

The Pennsylvania State University Press
University Park, Pennsylvania

Library of Congress Cataloging-in-Publication Data

Balestracci, Duccio.
  [Zappa e la retorica. English]
  The renaissance in the fields : family memoirs of a fifteenth-century Tus-
can peasant / Duccio Balestracci ; translated by Paolo Squatriti and Betsy
Merideth ; with an introduction by Edward Muir.

       p.   cm.
  Includes bibliographical references and index.
  ISBN 0-271-01878-X (alk. paper)
  ISBN 0-271-01879-8 (pbk. : alk. paper)
  1. Agriculture—Economic aspects—Italy—Tuscany—History—Sources.
2. Agriculture—Italy—Tuscany—Accounting—History—Sources.   3.
Peasantry—Italy—Tuscany—History—Sources.   4. Del Massarizia family.
I. Title.
HD1975.T8B3513   1999
338.1'0945'5—dc21   98-41052
                                                                          CIP

Originally published in Italy as *La zappa e la retorica: Memorie familiari di un contadino toscano del Quattrocento* in 1984 by Libreria Salimbeni, Firenze. Copyright © 1984 Libreria Salimbeni.

This English translation, an abridged and revised version of the original Italian edition, first published in 1999 by The Pennsylvania State University Press, University Park, PA 16802-1003. Copyright © 1999 The Pennsylvania State University

Frontispiece: The Flight into Egypt by Giovanni di Paolo (c. 1400–1482). Pinacoteca Nazionale, Sien

This book is
for Valentina and Ornella

The translation is for Giacomo and Miranda,
whose cries accompanied the labor.

History does not exist. Perhaps you think the generations of leaves that have dropped from that tree, autumn after autumn, still exist? The tree exists; its new leaves exist; but these leaves will also fall; in time, the tree itself will disappear—in smoke, in ashes. A history of those leaves? A history of that tree? Nonsense! If every leaf were to write its history, if the tree were to write its history, then we would say, "Ah, yes, this is history." . . . Your grandfather, did he write his history? Or your father? Or mine? Or our great-grandfathers or our great-great-grandfathers? They went down into the earth to rot, no more and no less, like the leaves, and they left no history of themselves. . . . The tree is still there, yes, and we are its new leaves. And we will fall too. . . . The tree that will remain, if it does remain, can also be sawed down, limb by limb: kings, viceroys, popes, generals, the great ones, that is. . . . What we are making, you and I, is a little fire, a little smoke with these limbs, in order to beguile people, whole nations—every living human being. . . . History! What about my father? What about your father? And the rumbling of their empty bellies, the voice of their hunger? Do you believe this will be heard in history? That there will be a historian with an ear keen enough to hear?

Leonardo Sciascia, *The Council of Egypt*

Contents

Introduction by Edward Muir   ix

Introduction by Duccio Ballestracci   xvii

1. A Region with Pen in Hand   1

2. "Luscious Valleys" and "Magnificent Villas"   11

3. A Village Bourgeoisie   23

4. A Peasant Saga: Nanni, Meo, Giovanni, and Galgano   33

5. The Story of a Peasant: Benedetto   45

6. The Women of the Household   63

7. Cultivation and Animal Husbandry   71

8. The Lime Kiln   83

9. A Family Confronts the State   89

10. Exit from History   97

Appendix   101

Notes   115

Index   139

Introduction by Edward Muir

We cannot know our ancestors. They are dead, gone, forever lost to memory except in the genes we carry and a few surviving fragments of information about their lives—perhaps some important legal papers, a family heirloom, some stories passed down, or rarely something as intimate as private letters or a diary. These fragments tell us little or nothing about what really mattered, the intimate things they said to their lovers, their hopes for their children, or how they escaped starvation in bad times. These fragments seldom date back more than two or three generations and have most likely survived more by accident than design. Even that most obvious of fragments, our surname, tells little: surnames have been in use for only a few centuries and at best memorialize a thin ancestral thread, the fathers of our fathers, ignoring the mothers of our mothers and the fathers of our mothers. For many Americans, moreover, surnames are very recent fabrications, a label borrowed from a slave owner, a word misunderstood by an immigration clerk, or an identity invented by a grandparent determined to become something other than he or she had been.

Besides the one certain fact about our ancestors—that they all had children—one thing is highly likely. Most of them for the last 12,000 years or so were probably farmers. Although we might not know anything about their fears and hopes or even their names, we can learn something about the habitual activity of farming that occupied most of their time, season after season, year after year, across the millennia. We can begin to appreciate something about their intimacy with the dirt, animals, sweat, and skills of farming that made their survival and our existence possible. Whether they originally came from Asia, Africa, or Europe, our ancestors shared a common experience of living and working in farming villages. Until very recently that was the common lot of most of humankind.

Our ignorance of these people is why Duccio Balestracci begins this book with the startling quotation from the late Leonardo Sciascia: "history does not exist." We cannot hear "the rumbling of [our fathers'] empty bellies, the voice of their hunger." Sciascia, a brilliant novelist who wrote detective stories in which the crime is never solved, asked rhetorically if there "will be a historian with an ear keen enough to hear?" Duccio Balestracci is just that historian.

Balestracci allows us to hear the rumblings of the empty ancestral belly because of the serendipitous survival of two parchment-bound farming diaries found in the Archive of the Society of the Executors of Pious Dispositions in Siena, a medium-sized city in Tuscany, a region of central Italy. These two little books are filled with writings in many different hands that date from 1439 to 1502, in other words from the peak of the Renaissance, the age of the Medici, Michelangelo, and Machiavelli. Siena lies some fifty miles south of Florence, the center of the Renaissance, and boasted a vital cultural life of its own.

These books make an otherwise anonymous peasant family knowable, in large part because of the obsession of Italian Renaissance culture with the written word. The books contain records of the mundane transactions—"today I received 30 lire for a young heifer I sold"—of a family who lived just outside of Siena and who were, remarkably enough, themselves illiterate: they had to have others keep their farming diary for them. The simple words of these simple peasant farmers represent the lost voices of all our forefathers and foremothers.

Because Benedetto del Massarizia was the most diligent member of his family in keeping the diary, he is the principal character of the story. Relatively prosperous in comparison to his brother, cousin, and neighbors, Benedetto worked his own fields but also rented and sharecropped other small plots, sometimes at some distance from one another. Simultaneously a landlord and a tenant, Benedetto was both a man of property and a man who worked for others. He regularly participated in the lively local land market, buying fields on credit from lenders in the city of Siena and enjoying income from the land before it was repossessed.

One of the most notable findings from the diaries is the role of sharecropping in Benedetto's activities. In the world of fifteenth-century Tuscany, peasants could either rent a field from a landlord for a fixed annual fee or become a sharecropper by splitting the produce from the fields with the landlord, usually giving him half the crop in a system called *mezzadria*. Historians and agricultural reformers have long considered sharecropping a highly exploitative agricultural system because by taking half of everything produced, landlords prevented peasants from accumulating the rewards of their labor. With all initiative stifled, sharecroppers found it nearly impossible to climb out of a state of degraded poverty.

Benedetto, however, did not see sharecropping that way. Although he was already a small proprietor in his own right, Benedetto also voluntarily became a sharecropper in order to use the modest income from sharecropping to protect his own land from creditors. He used sharecropping, in effect, as income insurance and preferred sharecropping to renting land because sharecropping provided him with some form of protection during hard times. If the crop failed or rampaging soldiers looted his barns, he would owe the landlord only half of what was left rather than some fixed amount he might find difficult to pay. Far from a passive, exploited peasant who was tied to an ancestral plot of land, Benedetto was a crafty businessman who held his own with powerful landlords and with the moneymen of the big city.

As a farmer, Benedetto engaged in a bewildering variety of tasks on many separate plots of land devoted to different kinds of crops. He harvested wheat and other grains, made wine from his vineyards, pruned fruit and olive trees, and exploited woodlands, which provided pasture for pigs, fuel for his lucrative lime kiln, and firewood for sale and for his wife's cooking fire. He kept a garden for vegetables, raised chickens and sheep, had a horse and a mule, and owned plow teams of oxen. Everyone in the family participated in the farm work, including the children and women.

Less is known about the women in Benedetto's family than the men, simply because the farming diary records less about their work. Benedetto was married twice. His first wife, Mariana, is known only because of a notation in the diary about her death. His second wife, Giovanna, quarreled with him and at one point left him, apparently to return to her parents. In the absence of more concrete knowledge, we can only conjecture about the lives of these women based on the general characteristics of Tuscan peasants during the fifteenth century: Benedetto probably married Mariana and Giovanna when they were in their late teens, they brought a modest dowry to the marriage (usually a sum of money), and while married they lived in a seemingly perpetual cycle of pregnancies, childbirth, and nursing.[1] These marriages had nothing to do with falling in love but were arranged by the senior men of the families after a careful calculation of probable advantages to be gained by creating an alliance and transferring wealth between families. The location of the families' respective lands, the size of the bride's dowry, the expectation that the bride would bear healthy children, and the prosperity of the groom weighed most heavily in the calculation. Benedetto and his two wives had at least two daughters and five sons who survived infancy. Although after Benedetto's death one of his sons continued in the wine trade, the boys did not keep up the diary, their fortunes declined, and they eventually lost what Benedetto had accumulated, and to a large extent lost, with so much toil and worry.

Despite his relative prosperity Benedetto had to struggle constantly to keep from sinking into the abject poverty that surrounded him. Benedetto's father, Meo, and uncle, Nanni, had jointly bought some land, a legacy that tied Benedetto in numerous farming ventures and land deals to his brother Galgano and his first cousin Giovanni. Something of a ne'er-do-well, Galgano left his widow so impoverished that Benedetto had to bail her out and provide her daughter with a modest dowry.

Cousin Giovanni apparently shared Benedetto's enterprising nature, but like Galgano he fell deeply into debt. Giovanni and his wife Cristofana had at least fourteen children, eleven of whom were daughters. Giovanni was obliged to provide dowries for these daughters, an obligation that dissipated his resources and broke up his land holdings because he had to sell land to raise the dowry money, making it impossible for his three sons to put together a coherent farm. The dowry system, which led to the exchange of property and wives among peasant families, placed a disastrous burden on couples like Giovanni and Cristofana who had more daughters than sons. Moreover, if a husband died before his wife, as was the case with one of Benedetto's sons, the wife's dowry had to be restored when she returned to her parents, a situation that often put a severe strain on the survivors in the husband's family.

The peasants of fifteenth-century Tuscany shared with untold millions of other peasant families their position of economic and cultural subordination. Peasants were subordinate to landlords, bankers and moneylenders in the city, judges who settled their disputes, tax collectors of the state, priests who collected tithes, and all those who possessed the essential prerequisite of power—literacy, the ability to preserve memory through writing. The cumulative effect of this subordination has led scholars to classify peasants as *subalterns*, a term borrowed from military jargon meaning "of inferior rank." A subaltern class is, by definition, a group deprived of formal access to the institutions of political power, which protect the economic interests of the dominant classes. Subalterns are also excluded from the cultural sources of power, including formal education, literacy, and access to information. The subordination, deprivation, and exclusion of subalterns betray the hegemonic impulse of the dominant classes, the desire to control all aspects of life, all sources of wealth and power, all means of understanding and disseminating ideas, all alternatives that might threaten their own exclusive domination.

In fifteenth-century Tuscany the cultural hegemony over the subaltern classes, to employ the ungainly jargon of social analysis, meant that peasants who knew only a local dialect could not speak the language of power, and peasants who were illiterate could not record their transactions for future consultation. Illiteracy put them at the mercy of the literate who had the majesty of the state behind them. The impulse of the Massarizia family to keep a diary, despite the fact that they could not themselves write it, represents an astonishing attempt to escape the restrictions of a subaltern status. The Massarizia farming diary exemplifies what James C. Scott has called the "weapons of the weak," those many stratagems employed to defend the interests of subalterns against the seemingly overwhelming power of the dominant classes.[2] One of the great advantages of looking closely at the actual lives of such peasants as the Massarizia family is that it shows how the hegemony of the dominant classes was never as total as it might otherwise seem. As Benedetto's career illustrates, even an illiterate peasant could use literacy as his weapon.

Benedetto del Massarizia did not keep his farming diary because he wanted his progeny to know something of his life but because he wanted a record of his dealings—of the land he bought, the wine he sold, the money he owed and was owed, the dowries obtained—in order to protect himself from fraud and disagreements. Unable to write himself, Benedetto lived in the midst of an intensely literate culture in which virtually every transaction was recorded by a notary. Notaries in Renaissance Italy were the priests of practical literacy, the professionals who held the reigns of power over memory. When, let us say, a farmer from the country sold a pig to a shoemaker in the city of Siena, the two would contract the deal by visiting one of the many local notaries who would write up a record of the agreement in a large register of transactions he kept in his office. If later there were some dispute over the deal—either the pig was found to be sick or the shoemaker failed to pay on time—both parties could rely on the notary to supply a record of the exact terms of the contract. When Benedetto struck a bargain he went to a notary like everyone else to write up the contract, but he also brought along his little book and asked the notary, a witness, or whomever was available to write down the date and terms of the deal. In the course of his working life, Benedetto employed at least thirty different notaries who recorded the affairs of this ambitious, struggling farmer. In this way, Benedetto had a way of later finding the proper page in the notary's register for the record of his transaction, and he had his own memorandum of his affairs. Unable to write, Benedetto seems to have possessed enough knowledge of letters to be able to read the entries in his books, but no matter what his level of skill, Benedetto's two little books reveal the spreading power of literate culture associated with the Italian Renaissance, a power so keen that even a small-time farmer felt obliged to participate in it, bringing some small fragment of the refined culture of the Renaissance into the callused hands of a man of the fields.

Because he had a very practical need to break the bonds of illiteracy, Benedetto and his family have escaped the anonymity of the subaltern classes that made them a people without a history. Benedetto was a thoroughly unexceptional man, but the fortuitous survival of his two little books has made it possible for us to have a glimpse into the lives of all those unexceptional men and women, our unexceptional ancestors, who remain without a history.

Introduction by Duccio Balestracci

The subjects of historical research have undergone a noticeable change in the last forty years. Certain categories, groups, and classes used to be considered "without history" because they did not, for the most part, leave written documents behind. As recently as 1967 the Italian historian Giovanni Cherubini observed that historians tended to concern themselves predominantly with the ruling classes; he went on to note that "the life of the masses is in large measure unknown, and until these hundreds of thousands, indeed millions, of people show their faces completely, our image of the past will be incomplete and distorted."[1]

Only ten years later, Arnaldo Momigliano declared that the "most pervasive characteristic of the historiography of the past fifteen years is perhaps the focus on oppressed or minority groups within advanced civilizations: women, children, slaves, people of color or, more simply, heretics, peasants, laborers. This trend is compounded by a growing attention to cultural forms associated with the subaltern classes (as categories of powerless people are called): popular culture, magic, folklore, and, to a certain extent, oral tradition."[2]

Although historians have begun to attend to the subaltern classes, until now urban subaltern classes have been more prominent, mostly because it is easier to find written evidence on them. Within Italian historiography, the bias of urbanocentrism has also played a role. Thus, while the urban poor and the paid workers of cities have been revived, rural peasants, wage-earners, village craftsmen, servants, millers, middlemen, rural wet nurses, weavers, and washerwomen, shepherds, traveling salesmen, and many other figures who inhabited the world of the fields have been forgotten. These people left even paler written tracks than the urban subalterns and have consequently been grouped together as if they were a homogeneous and undifferentiated mass.

Interest in agriculture is a relatively new development among historians. Nowadays we know something of crop yields and rotations and varieties, but we still know very little about the people who worked in the fields. How did they live? How did they think? What did they believe in and fear? As one considers the many unanswered questions, it is apparent that the few things that *are* known have been generalized to encompass and homogenize the entire rural world. It is as if, once outside the city gates, society lost all its complexity and nuance.

The historiography of contemporary times has benefited from the "rediscovery" of the rural world by ethnologists, anthropologists, and scholars of folk traditions. Yet for less recent periods, we are still little beyond the realization that generalizations about the countryside are unsatisfactory. The means by which to overcome this situation, however, are not abundantly available. As Carlo Ginzburg has observed, "Since historians are unable to converse with the peasants of the sixteenth century (and, in any case, there is no guarantee that they would understand them), they must depend almost entirely on written sources (and possibly archaeological evidence). These are doubly indirect, for they are *written*." [3] And, just as in a distorting mirror, direct contact with a peasant's testimony of himself, without intermediaries, ends up being an elusive goal. [4]

Thus, a book of accounts kept by a peasant of the fifteenth century is not a common thing, given how rare it is to find firsthand testimony of any kind from someone who lived in the world of the fields. [5] The account that follows is also uncommon because the two booklets upon which this book is based were kept by a man who may have been able to read, but did not know how to write. Furthermore, in Siena, unlike other Tuscan cities, private account books from the Middle Ages have almost all disappeared.[6] But the custom of keeping such books did exist in Siena: in the pages of Benedetto del Massarizia, the peasant protagonist of this story and owner of the booklets used here, one can catch glimpses of some thirty other account books and diaries kept by Sienese people. Leaving out account books kept by government officials, Benedetto's booklets reveal the existence of other such books kept by his contemporaries: a butcher, five cloth peddlers, a silk spinner, a shoe maker, five bankers and moneylenders, a barrelmaker, two saddlemakers, two clothiers, two woolworkers, a master woodworker, a shopkeeper, a goldsmith, a cloth cutter, and five other people whose trade and status are not established. *Their* books have simply disappeared, lacking the value as legal documents they probably had in other cities.

Benedetto's books afford a precious opportunity, therefore, to reconstruct something of the life of a peasant without relying on secondhand mediations. Benedetto did not leave much of himself in those pages, but he did put down enough for us to attempt to understand who he was and even a bit of what he sought in life. Intrigued by the trail left by the two booklets, I began a hunt for the peasant from Marciano, the village outside Siena where Benedetto was based, through other documents. Benedetto left informative traces of his life in the brief transcripts of his contracts in the registry office (*Gabella*) of Siena and in his declarations of taxable worth.

This book was created as a rather eccentric biography. The protagonist was not a person who "made history," nor was he one of those subalterns who managed to leave behind some extraordinary sign of his existence. Benedetto did nothing exceptional in his whole life. He lived as so many others like him did, but he also desired to keep some account of his life.

As I discovered the banality of his everyday life, I began to have doubts about the value of my investigation. Was I indulging in a taste for the useless? Was I only playing with the memory of a man? For me at least, the answer to these questions was negative. Rather, I was attempting to discover an individual within the vagueness that clouds the history of rural people. The story of Benedetto grew from the conviction that reconstructing the experience of one man, of his family, of his relations, was one of the possible keys to unlocking the history of the countryside.

Insofar as it was possible, I attempted not to represent Benedetto del Massarizia, his account book clutched in hand, alone in the deserted fields. Rather, I sought to place him in his environment, in his village community and amidst the people with whom he lived, spoke, and thought every day. It seemed to me that only in this way could his story gain meaning.

From the point of view of understanding the realities of the countryside, it seemed more useful to discover the experience of a village "bourgeois" than that of a poor starving peasant. The latter's story would have only confirmed peasant stereotypes, whereas the former's story demonstrated that medieval and early modern countrysides and their societies were not at all uniform.[7] Benedetto, in my account, did not become a *new* model of peasant to juxtapose against the previous stereotype. Rather, the characteristics of a particular category of country people became clearer and more legible, though still only fragmentary.

The figure that emerged is full of nuances, difficult to reduce to stereotypes of peasant hunger, fatalistic acceptance of subaltern status, and endless undifferentiated history. My presuppositions still remained, but in dialectical alternation with a surprising richness of life, and especially an unsuspected dynamism. Here was an illiterate man who kept a book of accounts and who forced me to reconsider the notion, often held by historians, that the "world of writing" and the "world of the city" were inseparably fused.[8] Benedetto's story reawakened in me a doubt I had had earlier: is the pre-modern countryside truly an absolute "universe without writing" as is so often believed?

The world that emerges from Benedetto's books challenges other stereotypes as well. This peasant family lived, undeniably, by working the land. But they ventured into small trade and crafts when need arose. Because they lived in a village community, the distinction between peasant and artisan loses much of its meaning, as it did in Montaillou, the famous southwest French rural community, where "there was no absolute distinction between artisan and peasant, or artisan and ordinary citizen, or even between artisan and noble. In this part of the world everyone worked with his hands, and often very skillfully too. A notary might become a tailor, a notary's son a shoemaker; a farmer's son might become first a shepherd and then a maker of carding combs."⁹ People like these challenge the assumption that sharecroppers did not seek to cultivate any fields other than the landlord's and did not engage in activities that might detract from the land's highest possible yield.

Who then *was* this Benedetto, who was not starving but knew the troubles of those who work in the fields; who became richer and then poorer; who sometimes thought like a city person but without ever losing his "peasant mind"? More questions than answers remained when the moment came for me to deliver this manuscript to the publisher. How many others like Benedetto were there? And how many unlike him? How were they different? I will say, paraphrasing Roland Barthes, that up to this point I have said what I know, and now a phase in which I will have to say what I do not know begins all over again. Such is the cycle called research.

As often happens, this book owes much to many people. It owes much to the kindness and flexibility of Ruggero Lusini and particularly of Renzo Grassi, respectively president and secretary of the Società di Esecutori di Pie Disposizioni. They allowed me to move easily through the archive of the society. Gabriella Piccinni reviewed the manuscript daily and made a host of suggestions and advice, a detailed listing of which would be too long. Furthermore, Giuliano Pinto and Giovanni Cherubini gave this book a series of critiques, corrections, and additions that it would be euphemistic to call merely valuable. Finally, from Sonia Fineschi, I received advice on the criteria for transcription. Although this book owes nothing at all to Valentina and Ornella, nevertheless it is dedicated to them. That is, at times, the way of the world.

A Note on Terminology, Weights, and Measures

The *lira*, which was a money of account and not a real coin, was worth 20 *soldi*, and the *soldo* was worth 12 *denari*. Exchange rates with the *florin*, Tuscany's major currency, fluctuated, but during Benedetto's lifetime it was usually calculated as 4 lire, while the *ducat* was worth 6 lire.

To actually establish the real purchasing power of a medieval salary is an arduous project. It is impossible to know whether the declared salary is the entire income of the worker or whether, as often happens, it is only a part of it. It is similarly difficult to ascertain the market price of some goods: frequently our records state neither the quantity nor the quality of an item, only the price. The numbers below are therefore purely indicative. They derive from the account books of the Sienese hospital of Santa Maria della Scala, and from other records of that institution contemporary with the lives of the peasants this book describes.

Cost of Some Consumer Goods

two sheets:	7 lire, or 1.75 florins (1451)
a liter of wine:	1 soldo, or 0.014 florins (1451)
a kilo of wheat:	3 soldi, or 0.037 florins (1451)
a capon:	14.5 soldi, or 0.056 florins (1457)
a pigeon:	5.5 soldi, or 0.068 florins (1457)
a chicken:	2–3 soldi, or 0.025–0.037 florins (1475)
a kilo of fresh sea fish:	5–6 soldi, or 0.062–0.075 florins (1477)

100 kilos of charcoal:	48 soldi, or 0.6 florins (1478)
a "big" chicken:	7 soldi, or 0.087 florins (1478)
two eggs:	1 soldo, or 0.012 florins (1478, 1479, 1480)
a small barrel of tuna:	20 lire, or 4 florins (1479)
a goat kid:	21–32 soldi, or 0.262–0.4 florins
a flask of sweet Greek wine:	9–10 soldi, or 0.112–0.125 florins (1480)
a kilo of walnuts:	2–3 soldi, or 0.025–0.037 florins

Workers' Pay

Type of work	Pay/day in soldi	Pay/day in florins	Year
spread hay in the hospital	3.5	0.043	1447
prune the vineyard	8	0.1	1453
paint the walls (materials included?)	16.25	0.203	1466
heavy labor	15.54	0.194	1467
shepherd	3	0.037	1489
general rural help	4.4	0.055	1498

Ancient measures have been converted into modern terms even though such conversion cannot aspire to perfect precision because the conversion tables generally refer to eighteenth-century measures whose values did not correspond exactly to the medieval ones. With regard to surface measures, the *staioro* is considered 1300.75 square meters and the *canna* 2.91 meters. The *soma*, a liquid measure, was 91.16 liters (constituted by 4 *staia*, which was half a barrel or 22.79 liters). The *moggio*, a measure of volume for dry goods, was equal to 24 staia or 872.40 liters, each staio being 36.35 liters.[10]

To spare the reader the toil of chasing down explanations from chapter to chapter, I will explain here, once and for all, that *lira* was also an evaluation of citizens' taxable wealth and served as a basis for the distribution of tax burdens.

The *lira*, strictly speaking, was the number, expressed in *lire*, which determined the fiscal responsibilities to the commune of each citizen; more generally, the *lira* was the entirety of the individual *lire* which were gathered together in special account "books" or registers. Each time that a new *lira* was needed, at regular intervals, sometimes decades apart, the *Consigli* elected special magistrates called "bookmakers." These latter gathered from every head of household the evaluations or declarations. In the declaration the citizen had to make an accurate listing of all his goods, movable or not, "that is, the houses, properties, money, credits and debits, perpetuities, monopolies, rents, exchanges, cattle, grain, fodder, wine, oil and any other item in any way owned or traded or stored . . . wherever it was." To this list a note on debts and dependents was added. On the basis of this declaration, relying also on their personal knowledge of the economic condition of the citizen and on the testimony of neighbors, partners, and family members, the "bookmakers" assigned to each a general number (the *lira*) to represent approximately his income as capital, with allowances made for debts and for the expenses incurred maintaining self and dependents. The name of each citizen, with his *lira*, was then recorded in great registers which thereafter determined tax liability.[11]

Gabelle were tolls paid on goods in transit through the city gates or on the recording of contracts. The *Gabella* was the office responsible for obtaining these taxes and the *Esecutori di Gabella* were its officials, who gathered them.[12] The *preste* were loans, sometimes voluntary and sometimes obligatory, which the government imposed at specific times of crisis on specific categories of citizens.[13] Lastly, from the twelfth century the *Biccherna* was Siena's main financial magistracy. It was run by four *Provveditori* "who remained in office for six months beginning on the first day of January and July."[14]

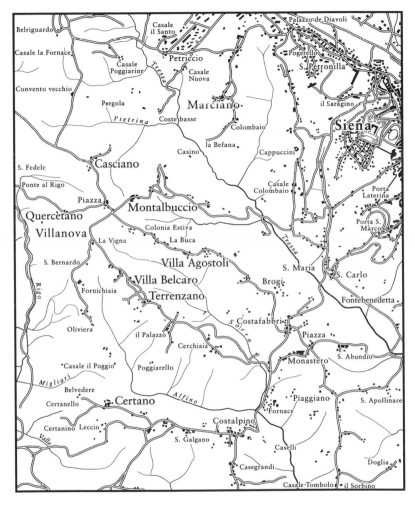

Modern Siena and the Masse Region

1

A Region with Pen in Hand

 At the end of the Middle Ages, urban Tuscans seemed stricken with a writing fever, a desire to note down everything they saw. Between the thirteenth and sixteenth centuries, merchants filled entire cabinets with notes on business transactions, family memoirs, and accounts of urban life. In Tuscany this phenomenon reached a level of sophistication and volume that makes other regions of Italy or Europe pale to insignificance.

The custom of keeping written accounts was born in the shops, whether the giant warehouse of a major trader like a Peruzzi or the modest workbench of an artisan. All of Tuscan society was permeated with the habits of the region's mercantile class. Indeed, the increasing use of writing to set down the business transactions of a whole family accompanied the region's economic development. The practice spread as Tuscan merchants became successful in Europe, and it signaled the great vitality of the merchant culture that rapidly gained political ascendancy in the cities.[1]

Pleasure in writing soon developed out of the pragmatic need to keep business records. This delight in handling pen and paper quickly led to the recording of matters of city politics or family affairs next to lists of income and outlay.[2] Perhaps memoirs took this direction because family and business were one, a single enterprise where diverse interests fused, and because the subtly narcissistic temptation to leave behind a trace of who one is or who one managed to become is so strong.[3] Or perhaps this happened because of the desire to take note "of everything that seems to me worth recording," as wrote the artisan Neri di Bicci, a painter and scrupulous accountant of his shop's, and his life's, business.[4]

While nearly all businessmen, big or small, kept some form of written memoir, this literary form sometimes reached the subaltern classes along with literacy. Among the account books kept by minor artisans in fifteenth-century Florence, there is even one, a "sort of diary," kept by a poor servant.[5] Similarly, in Lucca less than a century later, an illiterate tanner, a certain Andrea da Carrara, also kept his book of accounts but "because he did not know how to write," had it "written by a third party."[6]

The so-called universe without writing was certainly still prevalent in medieval Tuscany, but even among the lower ranks, and even outside the city walls, paper and pen were increasingly familiar tools. Written culture was not reserved exclusively for the ruling classes;[7] and in both the city and the country there were people who could write and read; people who could not write but could read (representatives of a culture in which reading is far more important than writing); and semiliterate folk, as well as people who had once known, but now had forgotten their alphabet.[8] Anyone who could read and write a bit was probably considered fully literate in the late Middle Ages.[9] It was not writing per se that was crucial, but rather "the comprehension of the content of a *certain type* of text accessible only through knowledge . . . of grammar."[10] By the sixteenth century, however, most semiliterate people had begun to describe themselves as illiterate although they were not entirely so.

They had been silenced by a "new hierarchy of graphic-textual values," which caused writing to become "an instrument far too delicate to be handled properly by nonspecialists." Only those who had fully mastered the skill and exercised it fluidly could now call themselves literate.[11]

But in the fifteenth century some peasants were still perched between the oral and the literate worlds.[12] The Florentine peasants who kept their papers carefully locked in drawers were hardly alien to the culture of writers and readers. Similarly, those rich peasants who took care to stipulate in their wills that their children be compelled to study, participated in literacy through their desire to use the tools of a culture that was relegating oral communication to marginality.[13] Martin Luther and Juan Vincent Vives had not yet pronounced "anyone who cannot read and write is only half a man," yet these peasants already sensed the utility and seductiveness of the world of writing.[14]

In the countryside, people encountered literacy along different paths. "Countryside," after all, has more than one meaning. There was one Tuscan countryside of isolated farmsteads whose inhabitants rarely spoke with people outside their families. There was another countryside of villages, close to the walls of a dominant center or remote among fields, whose social life was lively. In each of these countrysides, people approached writing differently.

People sometimes encountered literacy in a village school, an institution found in some rural areas in the late Middle Ages.[15] Often villagers included the demand for a teacher in their statutes, the constitutional guidelines governing the community.[16] To these people, occupied, but not brutalized, by work in the fields, it was reasonable to support a teacher "to teach reading and writing and some virtue" or "reading and decent behavior."[17] Sometimes schooling was actually subsidized: at S. Maria al Monte, near Pisa, it was stipulated in the late 1300s "so that men have the wherewithal to allow their children to learn knowledge and virtue, that no one who has begun to learn letters, grammar, or other discipline . . . may, or should be compelled, nor oppressed by any official of the commune, or by his emissary, to do any personal service, while he is studying."[18] Contemporary records from another Tuscan village, Castelfranco di Sopra, show that education was available not just to children; the community paid a teacher "who knows how to teach children and others who wish to stay in his school."[19]

These schools descended from early medieval rural schools established to instruct future parish priests.[20] They were sometimes run by clergy, but in other cases schools were staffed by lay teachers from the city.[21] If peasants could afford to do without their children's work in the fields, the children could learn enough to read a contract, to scribble their names at the bottom of a tax return, and to add up numbers so as to avoid being swindled whenever they bought or sold something.

Yet when peasants lived in isolation in their fields, how did they learn? There may have been someone able to "edify" them during their visits to the tavern. Taverns were places where it was customary "on the day and night of the feast" to spend some time drinking, gambling, or as the rector Arlotto lamented, "telling some of their dirty stories and lies."[22] Someone there, perhaps endowed with a slightly higher level of literacy, may have taught them something, brought them closer to a rough familiarity with reading, if not with full literacy.[23] After all, Menocchio the simple miller, well known to modern readers through Carlo Ginzburg's study of his cosmology, *The Cheese and the Worms*, was able to teach simply because he could read and write.[24] Thus it is probable that many peasants found a way, maybe helped by a priest or notary they met when striking some deal.

In the end, wherever literacy took root in rural Tuscany, it did so in the wake of notaries' writings; that is, of the contracts written by notaries to represent the interests of urban people. Notaries were the main mediators between written and oral culture, as written agreements, such as rent or sharecropping contracts, replaced the custom of oral compacts. Notaries also mediated when two mental attitudes, that of the urban dweller and that of country folk, were forced into contact, unless the peasant was willing to remain at the mercy of those who could make scraps of paper speak and, on account of this skill, give them legal value.[25]

Country people won a "victory" with the written contract, for it placed them on an equal level with the landowners. This victory was completed when peasants learned to decode the written signs regarding them and was crowned when some peasants decided to keep personal account books. We know of a handful of such peasants in fifteenth-century Tuscany. Fruosino di Donato di Gino, a sharecropper of Oderigo di Andrea di Credi, acquired a belief in the utility of keeping a diary from his landlord, who encouraged Fruosino by buying him "a small booklet . . . to write down all his affairs in."[26] Simonetto di Massaio was a Sienese sharecropper active in the 1430s who could not write but had others write "his booklet" for him.[27] The peasants Meo and Benedetto del Massarizia, the heroes of our story, much like Simonetto, could not write but asked others to write for them. These four peasants, though wholly or partially illiterate, learned enough from literate culture to begin to participate in it. Even if "hegemonic" culture remains removed from the culture of the fields, the curtain separating them is more permeable than it looks.[28] Just as some customs and tastes trickled down from the upper classes to the lower ones, so too did the taste and the practical necessity for writing spread to rural populations.[29]

It was not by chance that around this time Tuscany's city people developed a new insult for rustics. They had always been called thieving, untrustworthy, lazy ingrates.[30] Now they became *baccalari*, or "know-it-alls." This epithet was the reaction of urban landowners to these presumptuous bumpkins who, having mastered something of the alphabet, now used it to resist those who had previously overawed them. Meo, Benedetto, and all the rest with their "rhetoric learned on the handle of the hoe," were the irritating reminder of changed times.[31]

It is unlikely that Benedetto del Massarizia's intent in keeping his two booklets was to leave behind a memoir of his life. He had another purpose. His two volumes conform closely to the guidelines given by the etiquettist and social critic Paolo di Pace from Certaldo, who advised: "Always, when you have a document drawn up, keep a book yourself and write in it the date, the notary, the witnesses, the reason you had the document made and with whom, so that they may find it. This is to escape the many vagaries and dangers of duplicitous men. And keep it closed in your chest."[32]

That is exactly what Benedetto did. Benedetto had not read di Pace's advice, but he instinctively followed it. External events did not find a place on his pages: the horizon of his books was his household and fields. The booklets recorded things that were not necessarily the most important, but those whose traces could most easily be lost. Benedetto knew he could find a record of sales or dowry contracts in the notaries' briefs, or even in the communal register, whenever he wished, so he was not overconcerned with noting that type of exchange in his booklets. But he might not find any trace of his daily transactions. Thus, he compiled a book of receipts for the humdrum activities—for the purchase of cattle, for loans, for the sale of firewood, wine, and lime, and for the purchase of wheat. Occasionally a transaction recorded by a notary or some communal official also appears in his book; in such cases, he noted the volume in which the originals were kept with a precision that enabled me to track them down.

Family affairs appear indirectly, as traces left in his accounts. From the purchase of candles and funeral attire for the "burial of his woman," we learn that his first wife died, though Benedetto did not write down her name. We can learn it by other means (she was called Mariana), but in Benedetto's booklet she appears fleetingly only to justify the burial expense of 10 lire.

Similarly, the name of his son Mattia appears only because of the donation to the Sienese church of the Magione for his burial. Likewise, only the notation of taxes paid to redeem land confiscated from his brother Galgano (who died owing a sum to the tax office) informs us of an impoverished branch of the family. And when one of Benedetto's daughters got married, there was no evidence of the wedding save for the minute recording of expenses incurred to buy her clothes and to give her a small dowry.

Even in the instance when Benedetto had a conflict with his second wife, Giovanna, he was interested in noting only that she would have to return to his house and repay "earlier debts." He does not note the nature and amount of these debts, for he knew them. If he needed to, he could consult the original document, which "at greater length . . . appears in the file of ser Giacomo on page 235." Benedetto's book contained everything that he needed to remember: the crux of the issue, the name of the notary who recorded the settlement, the date the document was drawn up, the file in which the original document was kept, and the precise place in which to find it. He wrote down everything he might require, exactly as Paolo di Pace advised.

There is almost no trace of the family's lateral branches in the booklets. Benedetto's father, Meo, barely surfaces, although he may have been the one who actually began recording things in the booklets. He died, however, only four years after the first record was begun. Similarly, there is almost no information about Benedetto's children. Some scraps emerge concerning his brother Galgano and his cousin Giovanni, with whom, after the separation of the nuclear families, contacts were maintained. Some faint echoes reverberate of the marital strife with Giovanna and the desperate condition of his brother's widow and children and Benedetto's aid to them. They are, perhaps, loud enough to give us a sense of his feelings, his problems, even his troubles.

In deciding to keep these booklets, Benedetto, or his father, must have been influenced by the many urban businessmen with whom the Massarizia family had dealings. It is likely that some notary provided the booklets themselves, for the two volumes are very similar to notarial notebooks. They have the same paper pages, the parchment binding, the small latch to close the book, and one of the two bindings is made from the back side of a notarial document (cut in such a way as to prevent us from deciphering the notary's name, however). Benedetto and his family used the services of notaries frequently. Between purchases, sales, or dowries, they knew almost thirty notaries, and though they drew up only one contract with some, with others they developed a lasting relationship, almost like that with a "family lawyer."

Benedetto, who was the true keeper of the accounts, may have known how to read, but neither he nor anyone else in the family could write. He belongs in the category of people who were not utterly illiterate, but were not really literate either, and who gained access to writing through the help of others.[33] "Many sharecroppers and smallholders used their landlords or an urban neighbor, but most preferred to rely on less awe-inspiring intermediaries: the parish priest, urban folk who resided in the country, rustics who had moved to the city but maintained ties with their place of origin, or the small tradesmen who often had a foot in the city and another in the country."[34] These people often transcribed "feelings, states of mind, even gestures suggested by their rustic patrons."[35] The true author of Benedetto's two books was this army of anonymous spokesmen.

People from every social group wrote Benedetto's pages. The deep differences in handwriting indicate that they also had varying mastery of writing. Craftsmen and public officials, bankers and friars, notaries and clerics, aristocrats and school teachers all contributed, as did a doctor and Alberto Aringhieri, a member of the order of knights of Jerusalem, who was also an administrator for Siena's cathedral. Alongside professional writers like notaries or bureaucrats, then, we find people who were Benedetto's peers and hence awed him less.[36] These men held a certain cultural prestige in their social circles, which led others to make use of them even when they knew barely enough to scribble down a few characters.[37]

When both contracting parties could not read and write, they turned to such people. The grocer Pasquino di Giacomo records that he "made this writing upon request of the two parties because they don't know how to write." [38] A certain Giovanni d'Ugolino recorded that he wrote "this at their request because they do not know how to write," where "they" refers to Benedetto and another peasant from the Arbia valley. [39] Another example of the same procedure is Astorre Andrea degli Amadori, who recorded Benedetto's purchase of a pig from another peasant, paying his mother, who could only scribble her cross. [40] Writers wrote "upon request" and protected themselves by writing "they say they cannot write" of contracting parties they did not know personally. [41]

Everyone used the vernacular—Tuscan Italian. A few well-educated people, like the public official, notary, or doctor, used a little Latin for the date. Even those ignorant of the learned language probably had no difficulty understanding the small simple signs that marked day and year. [42] There was also a restricted use of Latin in the invocation, which began the text. A few wrote "Yhesus," and Christ was invoked by almost everyone else. Whatever the invocation or the style of dating, the vast majority traced a cross before writing text. They were following a deeply rooted tradition that invited the reader, and perhaps the writer too, to focus briefly on God before focusing, with far greater intensity, on what was written on the page.

2

"Luscious Valleys" and "Magnificent Villas"

 The life of the Massarizia family took place within the "Masse," a slice of country encircling Siena's city walls, about four or five miles deep, before the true hinterland began. The etymology of this rural district's name is uncertain, but the role of the Masse is not: like the *Sei miglia* district around Lucca or the *Cortine* of Arezzo, this area supplied the city.[1] Today this hilly area is so intensively cultivated that it looks like a jungle of agriculture. Fields planted predominantly with wheat are defined by a grid of vines and by irregular lines of olive trees ending in patches of oak woods. Poplars grow in the valley bottoms where small rivulets flow. The landscape is punctuated by cypress trees; as in much of Tuscany, these trees block the winds, mark borders, and, when close to the many farmhouses that litter the landscape (and denote dense population levels), just add beauty. Nowadays, some of the farmhouses show signs of nineteenth-century

restorations. Others are clearly older, deriving from the lordly dwellings of the medieval period, and tend to be towerlike.[2] But most houses reveal accumulations from the "continuous growth" so typical of Tuscan country houses.[3]

The city is a familiar backdrop to this landscape. Siena's appearance has only been mildly altered by the massive immigration of the 1950s and the erection of new suburbs. Seen from the Masse, Siena is a long wave of red roofs washing up against the blinding white of the cathedral and the pink stone of San Domenico and the Church of the Carmine, which mark the two farthest points in the city walls.

During the 1400s, when this story took place, Siena must have looked as Francesco di Giorgio Martini painted it in 1467: a crown of red bricks set in the green hills, from which protruded the summits of the rich burghers' houses, the grey towers of the aristocracy, and the tower of the palace of the commune, perhaps not the tallest of all but certainly the easiest to recognize from the countryside.

Benedetto and his family lived in this countryside. Their story was acted out between two symbolic poles—Siena and the Augustinian convent of Lecceto—and inside a triangle formed by the three villages of Marciano, Casciano, and Montalbuccio.

Siena attached itself to this area rather early. In the 1200s a "principal road" crossed the area. The Sienese commune, as the self-ruling city-states characteristic of medieval Italy are called, maintained this road, which tied Siena to Montalbuccio and then continued as a simple "way" to Casciano. Another "way" linked Marciano to the great Via Francigena at Santa Petronilla, the major route that led to Rome from the north and cut through Siena. Aside from these, there were no real roads in the 1400s, although there were plenty of paths through fields.

During the fifteenth century, the region must have looked rather like Ambrogio Lorenzetti's image of it, in *The Effects of Good Government*, painted around the middle of the 1300s. Regular fields separated by hedges of fruit trees composed a "safe" landscape over whose security

The Virgin Protecting Siena by Francesco di Giorgio Martini (1467). Archivio di Stato, Siena

the nearby city watched.[4] The area was dotted with landlords' houses, which served both as farms and as rustic retreats for their urban owners, and with smaller peasant houses made of earth or brick or adapted from old landlords' dwellings.[5]

Aeneas Silvius Piccolomini, the Sienese nobleman who had by the time he wrote his memoirs been elected Pope Pius II, declared that "this land positioned close to Siena is a spectacle of ineffable beauty. The hills are covered with vineyards and fruit trees, or are sown with wheat, and rise softly over luscious valleys in which both sown fields and meadows are crossed by perennial streams. Nearby are woods, some spontaneous, others created by man. In them, birds modulate their sweet songs. There is hardly a hillock on which the Sienese have not built magnificent villas. On this side you can admire noble monasteries filled with holy men, on that side the houses of private citizens, looking like fortresses."[6] Piccolomini's description certainly contains some rhetorical exaggeration, but it corresponds to the image of the countryside in both pictorial representations and in the more arid written documents.[7] When Benedetto's descendant Meo served as witness to an exchange of land at Montalbuccio, the notary drew a picture of this territory in a wholly prosaic tone in his notes, yet he described a wooded area of oaks, with poplars and cane thickets around the river Tressa, teeming with fish.[8] Several fortified monasteries encircling the region complete the picture of the Masse's landscape.[9]

The rich soil close upon the city had long been seen as the ideal habitat for "the classic Tuscan field with trees and vines, whose . . . features had slowly been formed by a centuries-long complex process."[10] This Tuscan field type's essential characteristic was polyculture, whereby several different crops are cultivated together on the same land. Polyculture, instead of wheat monoculture, was more common in the immediate vicinity of Tuscan hill towns.[11] The commons, those natural resources that a rural community set aside for all its members to use freely, were by then almost nonexistent, as were the pasturage rights that might have damaged the intercultivation of trees and grasses.[12] The Masse, like many hilly areas, was intensely cultivated due to the demand for food generated by demographic pressure and the presence of urban markets.[13] The Massarizia family bought, sold, and worked vegetable gardens, sown fields, vineyards, olive orchards, fallow land, and scraps of woodland, illustrating the variety and intensity of land use in the Masse.

The fields around Siena, the fields on which Benedetto and his family toiled, were characterized by a type of agrarian contract reflecting the mutual interests of landowners and peasants. It was called *mezzadria*, or sharecropping. It was very common in the Quattrocento, but had been invented earlier, in the environs of Siena and Florence around the middle of the 1200s, during a period when renting land had ceased to be profitable for landowners; it was supposed to use peasant labor more efficiently. It was also supposed to ensure self-sufficiency in food for both contracting parties.

In the sharecropping arrangement, landowners were supposed to provide the farmland and pay for half of the expense for "supplies," meaning tools, seed grain, and work animals. Peasants were supposed to furnish the other half of the supplies and the labor necessary for cultivation. The sharecropper engaged all members of his family, including women and children, in cultivating the farm. If a single nuclear family was too small for the farm (fairly common south of Siena in a region of "extensive sharecropping"), the sharecropper united his family with that of a relative, usually a brother's. Together they formed a "widened family."

In theory, the sharecropper's family lived on the farm, especially if the land was far from any settlements. Also in theory, the sharecropper undertook to farm only this land, so as to avoid depriving it of the labor it required for proper functioning. Again in theory, at harvest time crops were divided equally between the landowner and the peasant. Generally contracts had a short duration: after a couple of years the

Detail of *The Effects of Good Government* by Ambrogio Lorenzetti (1337–39).
Palazzo Pubblico

sharecropper left the farm in search of another where work conditions
and soil fertility were better (landlords, too, could seek new sharecroppers, more skilled and industrious, or simply more vulnerable and open
to harsher terms).[14] But of course all of these generalizations are subject
to exceptions. Reality never quite matched this theoretical image. Some
sharecropping contracts became ordinary rent contracts during times
of plenty, and some rent contracts resembled sharecropping arrangements during times of famine or war. If a farm were close to a settlement, sharecroppers sometimes lived away from the land, and in some

cases sharecroppers were permitted to hold multiple contracts at the same time.

Unlike those rent contracts in which the harvest was divided between landlord and peasant, the sharecropping contract required landlords to "invest" through their contribution to the supplies. For this reason medieval and Renaissance sharecropping contracts can be considered a halfway point between feudal and capitalistic farming modes.[15]

The sharecropping contract first appeared around Siena and Florence about 1250, and it spread unevenly through central Italy thereafter. Most of Tuscany (but not the area of Pisa) adopted it during the thirteenth and fourteenth centuries, as did Umbria, the Marches, and Romagna. North of the Apennine mountains only Emilia espoused sharecropping, and it never took root north of the Po River. In each place sharecropping's advance had peculiarities. Perugia's countryside witnessed the triumph of sharecropping only in the 1400s, when commerce and industry floundered and urban people sought in land secure investments for their capital. In the Marches sharecropping became established in the 1300s, in Emilia, despite some precocious signs of it at Reggio about 1250, it triumphed in the 1400s. Whereas around Perugia and Florence middle-class city people propagated the new contract, elsewhere, including at Siena, nobles and churches made ample use of it.

In some cases sharecropping and the investments of capital it required of landlords represented a "return to the land," a flight from trade and industry rather like what happened in early modern times. At Perugia sharecropping was a refuge for capital in a depressed economy. But elsewhere this was not the case. Around Siena and Florence the advance of sharecropping did not coincide with the economic "crisis" supposed to have begun around 1300, nor with the demographic, social, and economic mutations associated with the Black Death. On the contrary, Florentine and Sienese sharecropping became popular precisely at the time of the greatest mercantile and industrial development of those cities. There, sharecropping was a way to diversify investment, one that did not deprive other sectors of the economy of capital but complemented them. Apparently the main purpose of sharecropping contracts was guaranteeing self-sufficiency in food. Urban landowners tried, through this new contract, to protect themselves from the fluctuations and uncertainties of the food markets. Sales of products from sharecropped farms were always minimal, and the landowners of the Marches who shipped their sharecropped produce to Venice were unique.

Over time sharecropping lost its innovative edge. It began as a rational response to the need for more efficient use of the land and available labor, and to obtain reliable food supplies. But it became a closed system unwilling to incorporate specialized farming techniques (the only exception were vineyards) of the kind that might have led sharecropping out of its autarchic narrowness, responding to the evolving demands of consumers. While north and even some south Italian farming systems adapted their products to the demand of markets, seeking improved sales, central Italian sharecropping farms did the opposite. Thus, the innovative, progressive contract of the 1200s became a static, burdensome element unsuited to modern conditions.

By the end of the Middle Ages a variety of agricultural systems co-existed alongside sharecropping in the Masse. There were simple rents and smallholding by peasants and by urban people. Peasants who owned property, perhaps while also working as sharecroppers for someone else, did not always live in isolated farmsteads, which was the norm in predominantly sharecropped areas. Many of them lived in the villages scattered across Siena's territory.[16] These tiny settlements often grew around a parish church, or perhaps along a road.[17] Each had a mayor who represented the authority of the nearby city.[18] Marciano, Quercetano, Fornicchiaia, Agostoli, Terrenzano, Belcaro, and Certano—all villages of the corner of the Masse that concerns us—were already small communes in the thirteenth century.[19]

From an administrative point of view, Siena considered the inhabitants of these communities full citizens of the Sienese commune.[20] They paid the same taxes as did urban Sienese, and they were registered in the same books of fiscal records. They shared all the advantages and disadvantages of citizens. The advantages might include the right to negotiate directly with the government when forced loans were levied;[21] a lower taxation level, particularly important when Siena raised taxes in remote communities to weaken their economies and prepare the ground for a further advance of Sienese landholding;[22] and the "privilege" of carrying a banner, called a *palio*, of white and black velvet (Siena's colors) during the feast of Saint Mary on August 15, when other rural communities had to send their own multicolored banners, so dissimilar from Siena's.[23] As for disadvantages, the inhabitants of the Masse as citizens were obliged to make loans and payments more often than other rural dwellers.[24]

From their villages amidst the fields, the peasants of the Masse managed to find land to farm, shifting between different ways of farming fairly easily. The Massarizia family exemplified this in their movement between sharecropping, smallholding, and renting land, while some members of the family continued to live in the village.[25]

At the close of the Middle Ages or beginning of the Renaissance, the "luscious valleys" that so moved Pius II were going through a difficult time. Economic decline began after the demographic cataclysms of the mid-fourteenth century. The plague of 1348 greatly reduced peasant manpower.[26] In the 1360s, a further deadly blow fell on the Masse as many peasants fled the region to escape heavier taxes; it seems that their equal status with the Sienese no longer protected them from excessive fiscal burdens.[27] By 1378, the countryside was so desolate that a committee appointed by the urban authorities had to confront the situation, since "workers and other people who were taxed as subjects have taken refuge in Siena for twelve years, so as not to pay this tax in any way; and on account of this our possessions are all ruined and we cannot find anyone to stay on the land."[28] These were very harsh years for country people, both because of this fiscal pressure and also because of the looting perpetrated by mercenary bands, who did not restrict their robbery to areas removed from the city itself. It is not surprising that many peasants sought less dangerous occupations.[29]

Nor did the situation seem to improve as time passed. On the contrary, the abandonment of the country intensified. Population levels in the Masse may have reached their nadir between the first and fifth decades of the fifteenth century. In the 1420s, the government was alarmed that depopulation was continuing and that "many vineyards are being abandoned, especially in the Masse."[30] Into the next decade, exemptions, tax delays, and special provisions created a revival, but it soon became apparent that the structural problems were too serious to be removed by episodic legislation.[31] The fields retreated and the woods advanced here as they did elsewhere, even though this had been one of medieval Tuscany's most humanized landscapes.[32]

By mid-century, it was obvious that the policies deployed so far had achieved almost nothing. It was noted in the 1440s that the houses of the Masse "are lost and go to ruin. The closer they lie to the city, the more shameful for our government, and more damaging to our citizens who own them, is this situation."[33] By around 1450, the Masse had lost some 12 percent of its population, sinking to less than 16,000 in the period between 1451 and 1460.[34] Between 1400 and 1500, the number of households in the district of Camollia dropped from 245 to 10, and in the district of San Martino from 280 to 85.[35]

This luckless territory was also victimized by armies and war. Yet another conflict between Florence and Siena unleashed looters and fires right under the city walls, for this war was fought with guerrilla techniques and not regular pitched battles.[36] In the political chaos that erupted throughout Tuscany ensuing from the Pazzi Conspiracy of 1478, Florentines "oftentimes rode through Siena's lands robbing and wrecking everywhere they could."[37] The fates of men like Benedetto del Massarizia, who had "received great damage from the soldiers," or like his neighbor Giovanni Antonio del Feria, who watched his few belongings disappear, "burned on account of the war,"[38] were tied to the depredations that were the inglorious underside of a history which they neither knew nor made, but which happened to them.

3

A Village Bourgeoisie

Nowadays, the picturesque image of the peasant who lives in harmony with the land, caught in a changeless time whose only subdivisions are the seasons, is contradicted by histories of ever greater complexity.[1] Neither peasants' standards of living, nor their positions in rural economies, nor their familial structures, nor their minds can be reduced to clichés.[2] What did Benedetto have in common with a peasant from the malarious wilds of southwestern Tuscany? Or Galgano with a mountain rustic from south of Siena? They probably had no more in common than did Alberto Aringhieri, administrator of the cathedral of Siena, and Francesco Petroccio, the cloth peddler, simply because they both lived within the city walls. The mentality of peasants who lived next to the city surely was different from the mentality of those who had to travel a full day to reach its gates.

Perhaps there was a mentality we could label as "urban" and another called "rural." If so, the border between the two would not have been the city wall; it would have run through the fields of the Masse. Relations between the two worlds were regulated by economics, but they also intersected at the cultural level. City folk studied the fields outside the walls just as peasants observed urban cultural models, including written memoirs, and appropriated them. Even everyday household goods, clothes, and furniture in peasant houses often were borrowed from urban traditions.

Peasants' use of surnames in tax returns is another example of their appropriation of urban cultural models. It reveals an urban taste that probably reached the countryside through notaries, who needed to identify individuals with a less cumbersome system than a long list of ancestors.[3] Fifteenth-century Tuscan peasants rarely used surnames,[4] and when they did—usually for tax reasons—they yielded unwillingly.[5] Yet Benedetto's use of surnames was far from an imposition submitted to grudgingly. He designated himself as "del Massarizia" (which sounds like the Italian word for movable goods, *masserizie*) not only in public legal documents but also in his private booklets. The family must have found this urban custom a useful *sign* of their status, emphasizing their difference from their neighbors.

The Massarizias were culturally amphibious, in touch with other rural people as well as with city merchants and nobles. Loans, purchases, and sales occurred within a circle of people the family had fiscal, financial, and legal dealings with. Benedetto and his family called on all their acquaintances when they needed someone to witness a legal transaction. Thus Memmo di Mariano Finetti met Benedetto when he sold him a pair of red socks (he probably was the supplier for the whole household), and he was called upon to witness the transaction by which Giovanni settled his accounts with the Borghesi family.[6] Likewise, when Benedetto required a witness for a land transaction, he asked Francesco di Bartolomeo Benucci, whose sharecropper he had been years before, to join him at the desk of the notary.[7]

Yet this narrow world, composed of a small number of acquaintances who reappeared constantly at life's big events, could open up suddenly. It opened to faraway places when one sought a wife for one's son or a family appropriate to welcome one's daughter. The narrow world broadened even more, its horizons becoming wider than the commune of Siena, if a profitable deal could be made regarding cattle or grain. These peasants swung ceaselessly between city and country, and Benedetto's requests that notaries draw up his documents and scrawl notes in his booklets testify to his urban mindset. Whether or not this writing reveals a desire for social climbing, it is without doubt a sign of a tenacious petty bourgeois will, despite Benedetto's lowly position in fifteenth-century social hierarchies. At the same time, all the fiscal documents they compiled reveal the Massarizias to have shared the universal fear of dying of hunger. The few mentions of special, "urban" foods they bought (fish, veal) do not dispel the sensation created by their frequent protestations of penury.[8]

But rural people were distinguished from city dwellers, particularly by the fear of war. Benedetto, like his fellow villagers who suffered damage from plunderers, resembled all rural people. They might find soldiers on their land at any moment, and this created a vast distance between them and those who lived within the protection of city walls.

Thus, in spite of some urban characteristics, Benedetto and his family were villagers. Their slightly elevated social status was not enough to remove them from their profoundly rural roots. Still, their neighbors may have felt some envy for the Massarizia people, for almost all of them were less fortunate than Benedetto's folk. A glance at the affairs and property holding of two families in the Masse village of Casciano, insofar as the archives permit it, affords a comparison with the Massarizias, who constituted a village bourgeoisie. A couple of examples will suffice.

Giovanni and Bernardino di Antonio del Feria leased a farm with two or three staiori of vineyards with a cellar, a dozen staiori of arable land, and two staiori of brush. There was a hut, but it had been burned during the war "and it is a mess." Giovanni had a house surrounded by a tiny vineyard, worth 200 fiorini, and another vineyard at Terrenzano. Bernardino had a house on a small plot of land. The brothers lived pinched by debts incurred to keep some cattle for work and transportation, to buy iron tools from the smith, and to buy wheat because, as they said, they are "without grain and without bread" to appease the hunger of their families. Giovanni had ten "useless" people to worry about, including two marriageable daughters. Bernardino had four in his house, among them their aged mother. Giovanni resorted to pawnbrokers to feed his family and pay his taxes, or to the friars of Belriguardo or to Giovanni del Massarizia, who was no rich aristocrat but represented a "wealthy" person worth turning to.[9] In 1478 Giovanni del Feria still owed 19 fiorini to Giovanni del Massarizia, "the remaining portion of the debt."

The situation of Leonardo and Giorgio del Passara was similar. They owned five staiori of vineyard and eight staiori of arable and fallow land, together worth 100 fiorini. In their tax return of 1465, they claimed that although there was once a house on this land, it was no longer inhabited "because it collapsed and there is no way for me to repair it." The only animals they had to help them in the fields were two donkeys.

As time passed, their small property dwindled further. The vineyard, five staiori in 1478, was reduced to four in 1483, and three in 1488. Unless this was a clever ruse to cheat the tax collector, we must suppose that the families' economic troubles forced them to sell off parcels of the vineyard, which was their single source of sustenance. Inside their small houses, with their "few and worthless household goods," there was indeed no trace of wealth. In Giorgio's house there were eight people to feed "all incapable of work except for two." There was a seventeen-year-old girl, ready for marriage, but "for the time being I have not been able to afford her marriage." Six people "who earn nothing lived in Leonardo's house. Here, too, there were two girls of marriageable age. Leonardo claimed that he had to sell everything he owned to furnish them with a minuscule dowry of 25 fiorini each.

In both these houses, debt was an assiduous companion of everyday life. There was debt with the smith for the construction and repair of the expensive iron parts of the peasants' tools.[10] Debt was also incurred to acquire grain since "we hardly reap grain enough to last us two months of the year." (Yet these people did not declare their credits, including 4 lire owed by Galgano del Massarizia for some grain.)

The evaluations of the Massarizias' property made by the tax office confirm their image as the most well off family in the village. Their evaluations were the highest in the community for several decades. When the family first appears in records during the early 1400s, Nanni, Meo's brother, was the second highest taxpayer of Montalbuccio. His next closest "rival" was assessed at just half Nanni's 400, at 200 lire. The other assessments ranged between 100 and 150 lire.[11] The following year the situation changed. The tax rolls of 1411 show Nanni as still second richest, but his value had decreased to 250 lire.[12] What had happened is unknown but is not hard to imagine: some family member, perhaps his brother Meo, had taken his share of the patrimony and left the household to establish his own family.

When Meo was taxed for the first time in 1430, he was assessed at 250 lire. By then the family's earlier prominence had been lost: many Montalbuccio families were assessed at 200, 170, and 150 lire, a relatively homogeneous situation. Other people were the village "rich" by then. Pietro and Antonio di Vannuccio del Vannocchia's assessment of 1,025 lire would have made them middle- or lower-middle income people in Siena, level with the city's craftsmen. But for peasants, so big a gap between them and the other taxpayers meant that they would be considered quite comfortably off.

Meo's average position in society was maintained even when he moved to Casciano. Benedetto, however, made the great leap forward. His family was assessed at 1,175 lire in 1453, by far the highest in Montalbuccio. Some years later the respective positions of the Massarizia family's various households were well defined; the tax register of 1467

Table 3.1. The Taxable Wealth of the Massarizia Family, in Lire

Year	Meo	Benedetto	Galgano	Giovanni	Heir of Benedetto	Heir of Galgano	Antonio di Giovanni	Bernardino di Giovanni	Meo di Giovanni
1430	250								
1453		1,175							
1467		775	400	375					
1468		1,000	525	400					
1471		1,000		400					
1478		775	300	400					
1479		775							
1481	675			300		250			
1484		700		275					
1488		550		275					
1491				275					
1492				300					
1493		550							
1498							125		
1509					400		50[a]	100	150
1531					225			100	100
1549					180			175[b]	

[a] Lucia, the widow of Antonio.
[b] Heirs of Bernardino di Giovanni.

ascribes 775 lire to Benedetto, 400 to Galgano, and 375 to his cousin Giovanni.[13] Thus, out of the Massarizia clan, only Benedetto's family enjoyed a relative prosperity that grew with the passage of time. They owned land and cattle and had higher incomes than other families. They exhibited economic vitality and a desire to improve their economic standing.[14] In sum, Benedetto's was a family of the peasant middle class, whose prosperity was relative, fragile, always vulnerable and easily lost, but nonetheless very real.[15]

The everyday objects and household goods that the peasants used give some idea of their mentality. An inlaid chest can reveal more than any long disquisition the desire to own not only necessary things, but superfluous and even slightly luxurious ones. When peasants could, they chose to own the symbols of a modest luxury, visible signs that separated those in better economic circumstances from their neighbors. For example, sharecroppers of Oderigo di Andrea di Credi seized the first opportunity to buy clothes, ornaments, and other objects of some quality. Similarly Niccolo and his son Cenni had their landlord advance them money to buy leather belts, elegant shoes, sandals, and a "green garland, a comb, a pocket knife, a mirror, a woven bag . . . and a painted box."[16] Likewise, the sharecroppers of the monastery of Monte Oliveto south of Siena, always deep in debt, celebrated weddings, commemorated deaths, or more simply allowed themselves a more abundant meal at Christmas. They spent their last savings or took out loans so as not to deny themselves "at least once in a while the decorum required by the ideals and lifestyles then in vogue."[17]

Benedetto and his family shared this mentality. They sought a proper "external image" through the clothes they wore, the objects they used, and the fine furniture they bought. The Massarizia girls' dowries illustrate those "isolated signs of luxury" that they were not always willing to forgo.[18] An example is Bernardina's "practically new" nightgown, finished with "French-style cloth," not an everyday sort of cloth.[19]

The "pair of red stockings" that Benedetto bought in installments revealed their taste.[20] These stockings freed him from his traditional

Table 3.2. A Comparison of Variations in the Taxable Wealth of Benedetto's Family and Other Families in Marciano, in Lire

Year	Benedetto	Giovanni del Turco	Pietro and Iacomo di Biondo	Santi di Goro	Tonio and Pietro di Luca	Cristoforo del Sega	Francesco da Pianoro	Tommè d'Antonio	Cristoforo di Giacomo	Francesco and Nicolò Minorsi	Matteo di Menicone
1468	1,000	275	525	225	300						
1471	1,000	275	525	225	300						
1478	775	300	525		525	175					
1479	775	300	525		225	175					
1481	675	225	475		175						
1484	700	225	375		125						
1488	550	225	300								
1493	550	225	300								
1509	400[a]						100	100	150		
1531	225[a]									80	
1549	180[a]										80

[a] Heir.

undyed rough pants, the same ones worn by all peasants. Such purchases were rare in the family's wardrobe, for clothing was costly. (Even the wealthy Florentine architect and Renaissance man Leon Battista Alberti, who worried lest his belt be too tight and wear down the cloth of his suit, recommended that "one wear the new suit on feast days, the old one on other days, and in your house the most worn one."[21]) The Massarizia peasants dressed in an ordinary way on most days but kept fancier attire or ornaments for "solemn days." Along with the expected purchases of humdrum Romagna-style wool cloth came other textiles, light blue or green, unexpected concessions to fashion. Benedetto's pursuit of fashion and luxury reached its height with the purchase, probably in installments, of a "supply of a belt and silver and gold buckles."[22] These items told the entire village that the family not only had all necessities, but it could even indulge a bit in excess.[23]

Benedetto's house and decor would have made a similar impression. Most peasants slept on straw mattresses, since a real bed could cost as much as an oxen.[24] But in Benedetto's house there was a complete bed with "a bed frame four and a half arm's-length long and three and a half wide," with a mattress bought from a wool merchant and presumably not stuffed with haphazard fillings as so many homemade mattresses were. And the local carpenter who built the bedstead also received a commission for a "chest decorated with inlay three and a half arm's-length long" in which clothes and linens could be stored.[25] His new furniture cost Benedetto 52 1/2 lire, approximately the cost of a pair of young oxen or some seven or eight pigs. This was quite a sum of money even for a fairly well-off peasant, and indeed he paid for it over a long period of time, not in money but in lime. Nine years passed before the carpenter wrote out what seems to be the final receipt for the remaining 5 lire and 5 soldi.[26]

Without overinterpreting what little we know of this house, one can observe that this house and its decor reflected the social status and mentality of the village petty bourgeois who lived inside its walls. But despite this achievement, at a certain point Benedetto's fortune dwindled, from 775 lire in 1479[27] to 550 in 1488 and 1493.[28] When the three male heads of household died, the Massarizia fortune was already declining, and too many heirs led to its division and collapse. Giovanni's sons Antonio and Bernardino were evaluated at only 125 and 100 lire, respectively, in 1498.[29] Some years later their impoverishment had gone further, so that Bernardino was worth 100 lire and Antonio's widow Lucia only 50, the sum below which citizens were considered poor.[30]

Nor did Benedetto's heirs fare much better: by 1549, their lira was reduced to 180 lire.[31] Their neighbors had still less taxable wealth, but this is not important. The memory of Benedetto's family as members of the village bourgeoisie was now faded and dim, and to say that they were still richer than others would be a distortion. It is more accurate to say that the others were still poorer than Benedetto's descendants.

4

A Peasant Saga: Nanni, Meo, Giovanni, and Galgano

 The first member of the family to leave any historical traces was Benedetto's great-grand-father.[1] We know only his name, Ugolino, and his son's name, Betto. Betto, known as "the Massarizia man," perhaps because he accumulated some wealth (with a play on *masse-rizie*, or movable goods), left behind at least three sons. There were Nanni and Meo, and at least one other son, if the fiscal documents of the early 1400s, which refer to Nanni "and his brothers" (plural), may be relied on.

While Nanni and his family never left Montalbuccio, his brother Meo moved to Casciano before 1430; their holding may have become too small to feed two households, which happened often in the cycle of peasant family life. Most Tuscan peasants married by age twenty-five and usually could not expect to continue to live on the family farm, which, especially close to cities, was small and could support only small nuclear families of four to seven members.[2] Meo was back in Montalbuccio by 1430, renting land from an urban landowner; but in 1438 he returned to Casciano and paid a Sienese craftsman 60 fiorini for a plot including vines, vegetable garden, and arable land, with a house.[3] Two years later he signed a usufructuary contract (whereby he obtained use-rights in exchange for a refundable down payment and the promise to maintain and improve the property) with the friars of Lecceto for land at Casciano. Little did he know how much trouble this lease would generate for his son! This land, leased for 180 lire and a pound of wax per year, was taken "for the lifespan of this Meo and of his sons."[4]

In the next several years, Meo began systematically to buy contiguous small plots of land, a characteristic practice of landowners of this time. He began with the purchase of a portion of a farm belonging to the Sienese convent of Sant' Agostino.[5] In 1443 the friars of Sant' Agostino sold Meo another sliver of their farm.[6] Two years later, when he had absorbed part of the expense and begun to farm the newly acquired land, they sold him the last bit.[7] In only five years, the peasant Meo had amassed holdings worth the respectable sum of 400 fiorini. If this was the farm his sons inherited when Meo died, it was a farm made up of arable land, vineyards, and woodland, requiring five oxen to work it. Nanni may have contributed one-third of the purchase price, given that Meo's two sons and Nanni's son later shared ownership of the farm.[8]

By 1453, both Nanni and Meo were dead. From this time on, the stories of the three cousins—Meo's sons Benedetto and Galgano and Nanni's son Giovanni—diverged, though they shared a sense of belonging to a single group and lived close enough to each other that contact among the extended family was easy. For the remainder of this chapter we shall follow the lives of Giovanni and Galgano, turning to Benedetto in the next chapter.

Giovanni and his family always lived in Montalbuccio. As the main branch of the family, they may have taken over the family's original house.[9] We begin to know of Giovanni's activities with some accuracy only in 1465. He worked several plots as a sharecropper as well as some

The Massarizia Family

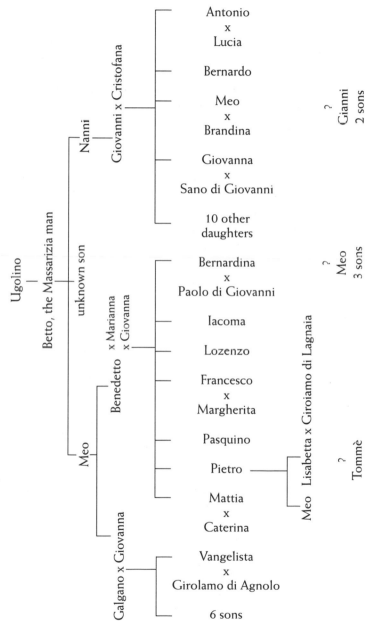

land of his own. Alongside this, Giovanni owned another plot, a "small possession of land" in nearby Villanova, two staiori of arable and four of vines.[10]

Giovanni shared business interests with his cousin Benedetto due to the joint management of their inheritance and the web of business deals between them. By 1453, Giovanni, Galgano, and Benedetto had bought a vineyard of five staiori in Marciano, complete with a house, associated buildings, and three vats for the wine, worth 130 fiorini.[11] But Giovanni never moved to Marciano. In fact, he probably received rent from his cousin for this land, bought when the Massarizia family was still a single unit. It is very likely that the following payments were part of this rent: the 19 lire and 15 soldi that Benedetto paid in 1469 "for eight lengths of cloth . . . which was delivered for Giovanna, daughter of Giovanni aforementioned";[12] the lira paid in 1471 "the change remaining of the 19 lire and 10 soldi [promised] much time ago to Giovanni di Nanni [his] cousin for a part of a dress . . . which Giovanni had for his daughter Giovanna";[13] and, lastly, the 40 lire which, as late as 1482 Benedetto acknowledged Giovanni "must receive . . . which money he must give to his daughter Giovanna, as I agreed to pay when we set out together."[14]

The climax of this business alliance came when Benedetto bought from the Borghesi family of Siena a huge estate in Marciano and paid a fortune for it, fully 900 fiorini. To meet this debt, Benedetto sold to Giovanni his share of the Montalbuccio property, complete with house and stable, worth 275 fiorini.[15] According to the contract, Giovanni would pay the sum in Benedetto's name to Tommaso di Mariano Borghesi, who would subtract it from Benedetto's debt. Giovanni stated to the tax officers in 1478, "About three years ago I bought from Benedetto del Massarizia, my fraternal cousin, his third for 300 fiorini, which, for the same Benedetto, I paid to Tomaso di Mariano Borghesi."[16] In 1478 Giovanni still owed two-thirds of the debt. As the Borghesi retained property rights on this land until the debt was paid in full, Giovanni paid an annual interest fee of sixteen staia of wheat and sixteen of wine for every 100 fiorini owed. Taking into account the contemporary value of wheat and wine, these payments amount to an approximate interest rate of 10 percent, the same rate that leasers of land generally paid.[17] Thirteen years after the drawing up of the contract with Borghesi, Giovanni was still paying for parts of the estate.

Perhaps it was to meet this obligation that Giovanni concentrated on his biggest piece of land, selling off smaller plots that only consumed time and money. In 1472 he sold the land at Villanova for 110 fiorini. As this was almost twice the value stated on tax returns a few years earlier, we may wonder how much a "shambles," how "thin" a place, and how "sad" a vineyard this "small" possession really was, despite what Giovanni declared to the tax office.[18]

Some years later, he sold another bit of family property at Montalbuccio to pay for seed grain. It was not unusual to be forced to buy grain. Sparse yields meant that a bad year left peasants in dire straights. This, as Giovanni lamented, referring to one of Siena's real granaries "is hardly a Valdichiana area" and "the harvests of wheat have been bad so half the time we have had to buy wheat." To pay for the eight *moggia* it took to feed the family, he sacrificed some of his inherited land.[19]

In 1480 a more conspicuous piece was lost when Giovanni sold a plot of land in Montalbuccio.[20] At that point, he owned one-third of the house in Montalbuccio, formerly Nanni's and Meo's, with its twelve staiori of arable land, two staiori of vineyard, and six of woods (he claimed they were mere thickets to the tax office) and meadows.[21] He worked this property with other people's oxen because in these latter tax returns there is no mention of the solitary "ox I have," which was his entire stable twenty years earlier.[22] He was, in sum, a smallholder who failed to realize the smallholder's dream: to reconstitute all the original paternal farm in his own hands.

Giovanni married a women from Toiano—Cristofana—in 1446, and eventually they had fourteen children. Although we do not know his precise age at marriage, if we suppose he was born before 1420, he would have been between twenty-five and thirty years old, slightly older than the average for his peasant contemporaries (which was nineteen for women and twenty-three for men in the early 1400s).[23] Still, Giovanni would have met with approval from Giovanni di Pagolo Morelli, author of a fifteenth-century memoir, who advised anyone who wanted to take a wife to "take her between twenty and twenty-five . . . but be careful not to make a disadvantageous choice in your hurry: I mean that if you think that by waiting until you are thirty you will improve your condition, so that it becomes far better, wait; and keep in mind that you should never let desire blind you in this deed, any more than in other deeds relating to honor."[24]

Neither do we know Cristofana's age. She may have been younger than twenty, as this was the preferred age for brides in both city and country.[25] This preference for young wives was to ensure the birth of sons "who may be ruby red, and strong and healthy."[26] There certainly was some age difference between the two, for Cristofana gave birth to a child every two years even when Giovanni was aging.

For the first ten years of their marriage there are no traces of offspring. This gap was probably due not to infertility but to a high mortality rate. Their children must have shared the fate of so many infants who failed to survive, as evinced in two examples from among Giovanni's contemporaries: Goro di Stagio Dati who had twenty-seven children, only nine of whom survived,[27] and Matteo di Niccolò Corsini who had twenty children, of whom ten died.[28]

Giovanni's first known son was born around 1456, followed three years later by a second one. As children, they contributed to the family economy by working as cowherds.[29] After them another boy, the last son, was born. In addition, Giovanni had a number of daughters. By 1488, he had married off seven of them but still had "at present four girls, some big, some small" in his house.[30] He worried about marriages for these four, especially since the dowries of the others left him in debt.[31]

Giovanni's situation was difficult and not uncommon; he had few sons to help with his farm yet continuous expenses from marrying off his daughters. Even the great contributions that women made to the peasant economy could not compensate for this unbalanced situation.[32] Indeed, if Giovanni had been a step lower on the social scale, some of his daughters might have ended up abandoned on the doorstep of one of Siena's hospitals, or even quietly killed at birth. This is suggested by statistics from the hospital of Santa Maria della Scala at San Gimignano, where 60 percent of foundlings were girls, and by the well-known fact of female infanticide.[33]

The dowries sharpened Giovanni's economic troubles. Having to pay a dowry, in conjunction with a bad year, an illness, or any unexpected expense put the peasant in the clutches of whomever had wheat or money to lend, usually at a high price. The lenders, frequently city people, often demanded household or farming equipment, or even the land itself, as collateral.[34]

So Giovanni del Masserizia fell into debt for "bought wheat," clothes, and other objects.[35] He had an unsettled account with Petroccio, the cloth peddler, "for several cloths I bought from him for my daughter when I sent her to a husband."[36] He had a debt with other suppliers for "cloth and other goods of ours."[37] The saddler Gaspare di Martino kept an open account with Giovanni, who acknowledged that "I bought and continue to buy," despite the 11 fiorini he already owed.[38]

There are no records of Giovanni del Massarizia after 1488. In 1478 he had declared himself "old by now" to the officials of the tax assessment office and had implied that his economic role in the family was entirely marginal, maintaining that "I can work little." Shortly thereafter Giovanni said he was "seventy years old or more" and, moreover, "sick."[39] These are the last signs of a man at the end of his life.

His scanty property was divided among his three sons—Antonio, Bernardo, and Meo. The "richest" of the three was Meo, assessed by the tax office at 150 lire. Antonio, at 125, and Bernardo, worth 100, were even poorer.[40] Aside from these fiscal details, we know little of their lives. Antonio, in particular, left few records of himself, though he left a widow in considerable economic difficulties after he died at about fifty.[41] The tax office assessed her at 50 lire, barely enough to ensure a hard life on the brink of desperate poverty.[42]

Meo married his wife Brandina before 1490, but their story is shrouded by impenetrable silence. From the records of a land trade in 1493, when Meo exchanged a plot of 434 "canes" of land, we learn that his family worked the land alone and dreamed of reconstituting a coherent farm from various scattered plots. Meo's land lay next to that of Giacomo di Leonardo, a Sienese notary who wanted a compact single farm. Meo served as arbiter and land measurer in Giacomo's exchange of land with a nearby landowner. Inspired by this, Meo traded 434 "canes" of his land next to the notary's woods for an equal plot of woodland contiguous to his own woods, and, in so doing, consolidated his holdings.[43] But after the 1509 tax assessment, Meo vanishes from the records.

We know even less about Bernardo, the poorest of the three. The only document regarding him records his sale of a scrap of land, one-quarter of which went to Benedetto, in Marciano for 42 fiorini in 1497.[44] Bernardo was still alive in 1528 when he was poor enough to be exempted from paying the forced loan levied by the commune of Siena.[45] By 1531 he was dead, leaving to his heirs a meager 175 lire.[46]

Thereafter no records tell the story of this branch of the Massarizia family. No public document from Montalbuccio even names them. Perhaps the size of Bernardo's inheritance explains what happened to these peasants: they cultivated small parcels of their own land but were almost surely compelled to work other people's land as well. They disappeared from history, silenced by poverty.

History has been more generous with information about Galgano, son of Meo and brother of Benedetto. This is due in part to Benedetto's obsession with writing down everything that concerned him, including those of Galgano's affairs that involved him.

Galgano was a smallholder. He, too, owned a portion of the inherited land in Montalbuccio and was unable to support himself from this land alone. In an offhand note scribbled in a tax return, Galgano recalled a debt he owed to Gaspare di Martino, whose "worker . . . I have been," meaning sharecropper.[47]

In 1453 Galgano married Giovanna, a woman from the distant village of San Martino a Strove.[48] Galgano may have worked his father's lands at Casciano, leaving Benedetto to rent some parcels right under Siena's walls. But when Meo died, their widowed mother could not cope with the Montalbuccio estate alone.[49] Hence, Benedetto and Galgano united their families and, as brothers often did, farmed that land together, splitting losses and gains until the moment came to divide the property.[50]

Sometime between 1465 and 1467, though, the two families split up again, perhaps because the Montalbuccio estate could not support two families. In 1468 we find Galgano settled on the Casciano farms, which had probably been rented to others in the meantime. This was the period when Galgano owned a "small possession of land" at Villanova, near Casciano, worth 100 fiorini; made up of arable, vineyard, cleared land, woodland; and endowed with a "large farmhouse," used as a workshop, in poor condition and roofless.[51] This "small possession of land" actually was *not* small: when Galgano sold it in 1469 it covered fully twenty-four staiori. The phrase he used to describe it to the tax collectors was a linguistic disguise designed to minimize his wealth, although there are indications that this land was not worth a great deal (the Sienese humanist Agostino Dati, the buyer, obtained a mere 110 fiorini from it when he sold the land at a later date).

Along with this farm, Galgano owned another in Montalbuccio, which he sold for 300 fiorini, twice its declared value, to Giacomo di Mariano Borghesi in 1476, "with certain agreements." What the agreements were becomes clear in 1478 when this land was still listed as in Galgano's hands, still evaluated at 150 fiorini, half its real price.[52] Rather than a sale, the 1476 contract was actually a mortgage on Galgano's land. The lender had demanded it as collateral and received interest on the loan through the land's products.[53] This situation exemplifies the way that city folk consolidated their finances by investing in land via loans to peasants.

When Galgano ran into financial difficulties, he turned, as other peasants did, to his current or former landlords. In 1478 he owed various people 50 fiorini, of which 23 were due Gaspare di Martino, whose "worker" Galgano specified he had been.[54] The human bond induced the peasant, in his difficulties, to turn to someone he knew, even if it would cost him dearly. A landlord would probably not impose the usurers' cutthroat rate of interest, but he would certainly obtain ample compensation for the trouble, although peasants had a customary "right" to loans from landlords for materials needed to keep the farm going.

Galgano indebted himself further to buy wheat. The Lecceto convent gave two staia for 20 lire, Cristofano di Guidino another two staia for 18 lire (of which 14.5 lire was still outstanding when Galgano died), and an unknown amount for 4 lire came from Giorgio del Passara.[55] Nor was this all. Galgano owed 40 lire to the blacksmith and one other person.

In his straitened circumstances, Galgano did what many thousands of his contemporaries did with their meager possessions. He took some objects to the Sienese Monte di Pietà, the pawn shop run by the commune as a charity, to free people of the need for usurers. Indeed, according to him, "Everything I owned, I pawned."[56] At the Monte, people pawned not only used clothes but household equipment, platters, and utensils and, in extreme conditions, farm equipment.[57]

Benedetto often helped Galgano during difficult situations, as his economic situation was less precarious: a sense of family solidarity, which could surface among cousins, was well entrenched among brothers.[58] This ethical code, requiring Benedetto to help relatives in trouble, was strongly rooted in the countryside as well as in the city. "Family" meant being able to take refuge under the same roof in times of trouble.[59]

Thus, Benedetto would pay his brother's dues for cutting wood in the commune's preserve at Selva del Lago, would pay Galgano's portion of their shared obligation for animals they raised on others' behalf, and paid the Lecceto friars the 19 soldi Galgano owed them.[60] When the two families divided, Benedetto loaned Galgano the money to pay off his creditors and launch a new phase in his life. As Galgano confessed in 1465, "I find myself with a debt of 24 fiorini which I must give to my brother Benedetto, who paid them to several of our creditors on my behalf."[61]

When Galgano died, it was yet again Benedetto who assisted his widow and children. In 1483 he paid the 18 soldi that the family of his dead brother owed the commune of Siena "for the recent forced loan."[62] He also settled an old debt of 13 lire that Galgano had incurred to buy wheat, a debt toward which Giovanna could contribute no more than a lira and a half.[63]

Yet Benedetto was able to combine his personal goals with family solidarity when he prevented part of the family patrimony from falling into the hands of outsiders. At his death, Galgano was in debt to the Sienese tax office, which confiscated and sold his land to recover unpaid taxes. But Benedetto paid the 90 lire needed to save the land and cover legal fees. He did so "since the possession of the heirs of Galgano di Meo, his nephews, was taken over by the Office of the Three Executors to recover the payments due, and since he desired to free this possession from sale in the best way he can." Benedetto paid the required sum in two installments.[64]

Barely a year later, and for a low price, Benedetto bought the share of this land inherited by Vangelista, Galgano's daughter.[65] Alone, Galgano's widow Giovanna could not cultivate this land, and Vangelista, on the verge of marriage, had no alternative but to sell it to create a dowry for herself. Far better, then, for it to change hands within the family, preserving the land from outsiders' interference while using the income it generated for a dowry. It is not clear where family solidarity ends and self-interest begins. But it is also unclear that Benedetto would have viewed the two as stark alternatives.

5

The Story of a Peasant: Benedetto

The real protagonist of this family saga is Benedetto, not only because he compiled the two books, but because he seems to have been the one most driven by the desire for earnings and a certain economic status. When he appears in the history of the family, Benedetto was already an autonomous adult. He went back and forth between the land that he rented or sharecropped and his own land, which he was in the process of acquiring. Upon the death of his father by late 1453, he became the head of the family: it was he who continued the book begun by Meo, and he who inherited his father's estate.

In 1438 Benedetto married Mariana di Chele.[1] He lived with her for twenty-one years, until her death in 1459, and judging from the dates of their weddings, Mattia and Francesco were probably Mariana's children. Then, at an unspecified date, Benedetto married Giovanna, with whom he also had children. With his second wife, however, all did not go smoothly, and in 1481 Giovanna and Benedetto appeared in court to resolve a controversy over economic interests. We do not know the substance of the lawsuit, but one thing is certain: by that time Giovanna had moved out of their house. The peasant, in fact, got his wife to pay him "the previous debts" and also to return "to live with me," as the notary who drew up the sentence wrote.[2]

During 1452 Benedetto was a tenant of the abbey of San Galgano. He moved onto the Godiolo farm at the gates of Siena, which was endowed with a house and a cellar, after living close to the farm but inside the city for eight and a half months while waiting to move into the rural house.[3] The Godiolo farmhouse needed some improvements, which Benedetto was expected to make, and which obliged him to live in Siena temporarily; his costs would be deducted from his rent when the bill was settled with the owner in December 1452.[4] He farmed this land with the intercultivation typical of this area of low hills; there is mention of vines and fruit trees. Benedetto's rent was paid in money, but the contract had the typical distinguishing clauses for the vines, in this case dividing up the produce.[5] Consequently, in addition to the monetary sum of 32 lire, in January 1453 Benedetto was to hand over half the wine made from the vines to the abbey in Siena. He was responsible for transporting it at his own expense, but the entrance tax into the city would be covered by the landlord, according to a clause quite common for sharecroppers.[6]

In the wake of the Black Death of 1348, the Masse remained lightly populated, creating a situation in which both sharecroppers and renters were able to find advantageous terms and hence moved around more than had been the case when labor was abundant.[7] In this case, when the accounts were settled, Benedetto deposited with the abbey administrator 1 lira and 2 soldi earned from the sale of "early grapes," leaving 8 lire, 19 soldi, and 4 denari still owed.[8] Finally, in January 1456 he paid up on this short-term lease—fairly typical, in its year-long duration, of this time—and his labor for the maintenance and improvement of the vines was factored into the calculations.[9] Moreover, the labor for improvements and maintenance on the entire farm, seldom paid for by landlords and, in normal sharecropping contracts, a cost that fell on the cultivator, were also calculated to Benedetto's advantage.[10]

While Benedetto worked as a tenant, he also owned land at Casciano that he had inherited from his father.[11] When he began to think of becoming an independent farmer who worked only his own property, an opportunity arose in nearby Marciano. There, in January 1453, he began to acquire land from some Sienese owners: five staiori of vineyards, with a house and a cellar with three vats. The whole thing cost 130 fiorini.[12] Galgano and Giovanni were also involved in the operation, but Benedetto was the only one able to manage this newly acquired farm, in part because he already worked some neighboring land at Marciano as a sharecropper.[13]

But Benedetto did not yet move to Marciano, the village where his interests seemed to gravitate at this point. Rather, he commuted from Montalbuccio, where he continued to reside after leaving Godiolo. He was probably constrained by the burden of his responsibilities to his aged mother and his family of five boys and two girls. "Since I want to support them," the peasant confessed, "it is best for me to remain a sharecropper, for on my own land I cannot support myself."[14] Unusual for a sharecropper (they tended to live on the land), Benedetto continued to live at Montalbuccio in the "poor little house" of which he possessed a third "due to the partition I made with my brothers." Around this he worked a modest piece of land, which was able to produce about four or five staia of grain per year, together with one staioro of vines and two of woodland.

Meanwhile, in 1465, in addition to the lands he owned and those he sharecropped at Marciano and Montalbuccio and Casciano, Benedetto, together with his brother Galgano, also cultivated the land of "La Cabella," near Casciano. These were "four pieces of land and a little unoccupied house, which I bought during my lifetime from the friars of

Leccieto."[15] In 1440 the abbey of Lecceto had granted lifetime use of this land to Meo, together with other lands near Quercetano and above Rigo, that formed a farm of both sown and fallow land endowed with a house, a cabin, oven, and courtyard (see Chapter 4).[16] This property was held in a type of arrangement, called usufruct, often found in agrarian societies during times of profound transformation, a system that was particularly valuable to early medieval churches and abbeys, which thereby created in the peasant a direct interest in the land he worked.[17] The Massarizia family paid 180 lire when the contract was signed plus an annual payment of a candle weighing one pound at the November feast of San Salvatore.[18] First Meo and then Benedetto (because it was lifetime right of usage transmittable to the heirs) brought the payment regularly, until 1465, the year when "on November 9, Betto del Massarizia brought two candles of one lira for both 1464 and 1465."[19] The late payment of 1464 probably resulted from the beginning of the controversy between the peasant and the convent over this land; in 1465 Benedetto planted twelve staia of grain here, but, he said, "They are weak and ruined." Benedetto maintained that farming there led more to loss than to profit, and he unsuccessfully proposed that the lifetime contract with the friars should be rescinded. The idea of that "weak and ruined" land returning to them, with the prospect of losing the small payment and of having instead to spend money in order to restore the land's fertility did not entice the friars: "I wished to give up this land to the brothers," lamented Benedetto, "and they did not wish to take it back."[20]

Thus began the battle of wills between the peasant and the abbey. In 1465 Benedetto stopped including the payments in his book. This was not absentmindedness; Benedetto probably reacted to the intransigence of the convent simply by ceasing payment, in the hope of inducing the brothers to back off from their obstinate refusal. The passive resistance of the peasant seemed to have some effect: in 1472 the quarrel came to the bishop's court.[21] In July, Benedetto named his attorneys, and less than a year later the case was argued in the presence of the entire chapter of Leccetan brothers, who, for their part, lined up an expert squad of lawyers. The two sides, in agreement, designated an arbitrator who, having evaluated "the arguments of the said parties and having heard these contenders over and over again express themselves in their own voice," pronounced the decision that, on November 29, 1473, resolved the suit once and for all.[22]

Benedetto was permitted to return the holdings of the Cabella with the lands of Quercetano and those on the Rigo, but he was obligated to pay the abbey the arrears on the yearly pound of wax. For its part, the abbey, obligated to repossess the lands, was instructed to return to the peasant, within one month, the 180 lire paid thirty-three years previously by Meo when he entered into a usufructuary relationship with Lecceto. In addition, the brothers would repay half the grain that Benedetto had planted on the land, and the peasant would be able to assert his rights on half the "grain and oats and other fruits which grow this year in the said possession." He could take all the straw that he harvested and was also allowed to cut "all wood for fire" in the quantity he was accustomed to cutting "and not more." He was prohibited from cutting the suckers from trees younger than five years and was ordered to clear out the cut wood from the farm within three months. He could not, however, cut wood in the fields along the Rigo, which "stay as they are, that is, nothing cut."

Benedetto was protected from the possibility that the convent would not keep the terms of the agreement: if by the end of December he had not been paid the 180 lire, "let him enjoy this property exactly as he has until now" until he had been entirely paid off; and, moreover, "let him not be obligated to maintain the buildings of said possession, but let them remain from the day of this award at the danger and risk of the brothers and abbey of Lecceto." The peasant, furthermore, kept a tangible pledge while he waited for the settlement from the abbey: if—the award established—the brothers wished to destroy in part or whole the buildings raised on this land (an obvious sign of the real "ruin" of these structures was that they were not worth restoring), they were permitted to do so with the exception of an "old hut" that was in the hands of Benedetto who, however, "had to maintain it," so as not to return property of inferior value to that received.

Finally, a last provision further protected Benedetto: if the friars "wished to pay the said 180 lire to Betto or his heirs, they should pay him six months before the harvest and then afterwards the crops would be divided" to spare the peasant from taking care of the fields exclusively at his own expense until the harvest, risking, then, the loss of this harvest. If this provision was not observed, "all the harvest of that year would go to Betto or his heirs, and the brothers would be owed the property without any fruits." With the agreement that each party would pay half of the legal expenses and of those for the registration of the contract, the controversy was finally resolved.

In spite of the group of prestigious lawyers hired by the abbey, Benedetto had essentially won on every front. He would return lands that were only a nuisance to him, too costly to maintain; and, if the 180 lire owed him had not the value that it did thirty years before, he had obtained a series of guarantees that protected him from last-minute maneuvers by the friars.

Compliance with these reciprocal obligations, however, dragged on a bit more. Only a year later did Benedetto enter the receipt in his book, signed by the prior of the abbey, attesting that on that day "the account was settled with Betto of Massaritia of the rent and of all other things we have done together and nullifying all other claims he had with the abbey of Lecceto, we remain equal and in agreement."[23] The Massarizia family would have further dealings for other reasons with this abbey, but the difficult question of the Cabella farm was, finally, resolved.

Benedetto must have been relieved, because in that same year he had also sold a piece of land in Casciano composed of arable land, olives, forest and fallow, valued at 80 fiorini.[24] Perhaps these fields were a remainder of the family patrimony in Casciano, which Benedetto was no longer able to manage directly. Nevertheless, his preoccupation both with ridding himself of the Cabella and with selling this other land seems to derive from a single aspiration: Benedetto was preparing for a great leap forward into the world of the small peasant proprietor. He accomplished this the following year with the acquisition of the extensive estate in Marciano.

On October 4, 1466, Benedetto and Tommaso di Mariano Borghesi —a member of one of the most notable families in Siena—appeared at the office of a notary to request a bill of sale for some land in the Masse, in the village Marciano. The estate consisted of sixty staiori of sowed land, vines, and fallow, plus a house furnished with five vats. The price that Benedetto paid corresponds to the conspicuous size of this farm: 900 fiorini, an extraordinary sum for a person whose taxable worth was 200 fiorini.[25] The property was divided into four portions, one of which remained with the Borghesi while the other three passed to Benedetto. These proportions were followed in paying the expense of registering the contract: Borghesi paid 30 lire and the other 90 were paid by Benedetto, who diligently noted in his book that "on November 7, 1466 I paid to Salimbene Petroni, chamberlain of the tax office, 90 lire levied for three-quarters of the property purchased from Tomaso Burghesi."[26] But Benedetto could never have paid such a huge sum, and because of this the two parties agreed to various installments and settled on leaving the reserved lands of the Borghesi to mortgage "until the entire price will be resolved."[27]

This was, perhaps, the moment of the enterprising Benedetto's greatest transformation. Faced with such a vast possession and such a heavy financial commitment, he concentrated all his energies on these new lands. He rescinded the sharecropping contract that tied him to the son of that Bartolomeo Benucci for whom he had worked since at least 1459.[28] On August 2, 1466, about a month before acquiring the farm in Marciano, in fact, Benedetto had to settle his accounts with Benucci, and the sharecropper, as usual, was in debt to the landowner. This was both because Benedetto had needed loans for buying seed, livestock, and other things before the lease officially began, advances which he found it difficult to pay back, and also because in this case there was no new proprietor to underwrite the previous debts, as often happened when a sharecropper went to a new farm.[29]

Thus upon leaving the old farm, Benedetto owed 6 lire, even after all his own expenses for tilling the land and the profits from raising the livestock in his care were subtracted from the original debt.[30] From this debt were also subtracted the hay, belonging to the owner; the newly planted trees, another fundamental aspect of his improvement of the farm; and finally all the gifts (payments of "hens and eggs") that accompanied the other clauses of a sharecropping contract in this period.[31] Immediately after this, the payments of the installments to the Borghesi began. These obligations left traces in Benedetto's book: 40 lire in May 1468, another 18 in June, and 34 halfway through this month, an amount that was added to the preceding payment—which Benedetto had not written down—for a total of 217 lire and 16 soldi (a bit more than 54 fiorini), as Onofrio Borghesi, who collected the installments, carefully noted in the notebook of the peasant.[32]

Some time later Benedetto faced the first difficulties in paying Borghesi. As was his habit, he turned to the person with whom he was most familiar among those in a position to help. His former landlord, Francesco di Bartolomeo di Guglielmo, came to his aid and paid Onofrio Borghesi another 73 lire as an additional advance; Benedetto succeeded in paying this loan back after some months.[33]

Such sporadic aid was not enough, and Benedetto confronted a hard choice: if he wanted to maintain the Marciano farm he would have to get rid of some of his other lands. In July 1471, he sold land with a house and stable in Montalbuccio to his cousin Giovanni, thus avoiding the dispersal of family property to external owners. Benedetto took about 300 fiorini of the amount paid by his cousin directly to Tommaso di Mariano Borghesi,[34] and with this payment another piece of the Marciano farm was definitely secured.

But even this was not enough if Benedetto wanted to stay on top of the payments for the Marciano lands. The only solution was to take on a second farm, putting himself—though he was already an owner—in the position of sharecropper to another man. On February 23, 1475, he drew up a contract with Bernardino di Pietro di Nanni del Besso for land near his own, conveniently cultivatable with the same tools and the same animals employed in his other fields. Bernardino, for his part, made "known and manifest to him who will read this book" that Benedetto took on the sharecropping without residing on the farm, but the peasant was committed to "work the said lands as a good worker, in good faith without fraud." The owner would not furnish the work animals, but "the said Benedetto, my sharecropper, must bring the oxen with him" obligating him, therefore, to own the only type of animal that did not increase in value, from which it was difficult to obtain some form of profit and on which, instead, loss was always certain. Unlike sheep or pigs, as working animals aged they depreciated in resale value and, during their lives, they did not produce usable by-products like milk and wool.[35]

Benedetto and Bernardino del Besso shared the expense of wheat seed, the grain that most owners sought, both because it was destined for the landlords' tables—in the city "white" bread was eaten—and because it could be profitably marketed in cities, where wheat was preferred to other grains.[36] The owner and sharecropper also split the hay grown on the farm, for fodder or for composting, while "without exception let all the stubble belong to Betto my sharecropper."[37] In contrast, the tasks of maintaining the drainage canals—the "fosse"—were entirely the burden of the sharecropper, following fifteenth-century custom.[38] And it was Benedetto's duty to take the owner his portion of the harvest "with his vehicle and my toll" (in other words, transport was at the sharecropper's expense and the entry tolls at the city gate were the owner's responsibility).[39] On the whole, for a sharecropping pact it seems more favorable to the owner than was typical in the 1400s.[40]

Benedetto's family, thus, cultivated two farms at the same time, a primary one as owners and a secondary one as sharecroppers. This phenomenon is not entirely undocumented; in the second half of the thirteenth century some city owners had let their extra lands to smallholders in sharecropping arrangements.[41] In fifteenth-century Tuscany, it was not rare to find peasants who, beside farming half of a farm, maintained a marginal property or took on more than one farm, probably because in a self-sufficient domestic economy they were not fully supported by a single plot of land.[42] They could also profitably redistribute and maximize the labor available within the family, perhaps aided in this by the landowners struggling to combat the scarcity of labor following the demographic crisis of the late 1300s and thereafter.[43]

From the early 1300s, even in so-called classical sharecropping there were exceptions to the obligation of working only the farms of the owner. In general, such concessions were made following adequate compensation to the landlord for the labor the peasant subtracted from the first farm.[44] But in the case of the contract between Benedetto and Bernardino, the situation seems radically different, almost, one might say, upside down. This is not a sharecropper who possesses another farm in addition to the first one, with both held on a sharecropping contract. Rather, Benedetto was a small landowner who added the revenues from a sharecropped farm to those from his own lands. Benedetto, that is, used sharecropping to protect his own land from his creditors. He worked the sharecropped farm as a "reserve." In other words, his strategy seems to have been to make the sharecropping relationship almost a "shelter contract," from which he would derive a small income that would protect him in difficult times. It is no accident that when estates switched back and forth between being farmed by simple lease and being farmed by sharecropping, sharecropping was the preferred type of contract especially in periods when peasants faced difficulties: thus, it was not unusual in times of war or famine to find renters who transformed themselves into sharecroppers. This was the only way of harmonizing the needs of peasants with the needs of owners, whose exploitation of their workers during such crises was consciously mitigated.[45]

Thus Benedetto, in a difficult moment, took "refuge" in a sharecropping contract that secured him a landlord who could lend him money or seed and who could assure him, however bad things were, land on which to work. "I entrust myself to Your Lordships, for we have received great damage from the soldiers," said Benedetto in 1481: here, when the inexorable moment of difficulty struck, a sharecropped farm was a lifeboat.

But the farm at Marciano continued for years to shape the life of this peasant. The infusion of capital from the sale of lands of Montalbuccio was not enough to stay ahead of the pledge, nor was the income from sharecropping. In 1476 Benedetto had to mortgage half the property at Marciano. Ser Giusto di ser Dino "bought" with a pact of retroactive sale "half of the undivided land" of Benedetto in Marciano for 400 fiorini.[46] The peasant was committed to repaying the sum in six years and to pay interest, which was here called rent.[47]

The interest disguised as rent was "thirty-two staia per each hundred fiorini": the peasant who declared it did not specify which products would go to compose the thirty-two staia, but considering the characteristics of a farm composed of "workable land and vineyard," Benedetto would most likely take grain or wine to the city "to his house [ser Giusto's] in my cart and with tolls at his expense."[48] Whether grain or wine was preferred, the interest could not exceed 10 percent; this is more or less the figure in an analogous situation between Giovanni del Massarizia and the Borghesi family.

Benedetto could recover the land one piece at a time and could "make many purchases" as long as each installment that he paid was not less than the value of one-eighth of the entire mortgaged amount, to avoid inconvenience to the lender.[49] The first installment of the repayment occurred three years later, in 1479, when Benedetto "reacquired" one-eighth of his mortgaged land, for the price of 50 fiorini (exactly one-eighth of the total), without any re-evaluation of the land. It was agreed, thus, that if the portion was estimated to be worth more than in the past, the increased value should be credited to Benedetto "as a gift among living partners."[50]

Meanwhile, Benedetto continued his policy of shelter contracts: the lands of Marciano still were a problem and he tried to obtain from a landowner some guarantee against adversity. In 1477, soon after signing the mortgage with ser Giusto and ser Antonio, Benedetto again protected himself against the chance of being without land to work and rented, near Marciano, a property of the Sienese church of the Magione, made up of arable land, vine, fruit trees, and with two houses.[51]

To work this land Benedetto had to cancel his earlier sharecropping contract. Yet to stay on top of all these simultaneous commitments, Benedetto must have had help from his sons in working the various fields. Lorenzo may have lived with him,[52] but another son, Francesco, lived at Monteforelli, which was a long way from Benedetto's area.[53] Mattia, a third son, almost certainly worked with Francesco because it was from nearby that he took a wife, although Mattia probably went to work around Marciano at some point prior to his premature death before March 1479.[54]

For the Magione's lands Benedetto paid 74 lire annually in two installments (November 1, when the year "began" for the contract, and August 15).[55] The payment collector for the Sienese church of the Magione was among the most notable personalities in Siena at this time: Alberto Aringhieri, a man with whom the Massarizia family had many dealings, who was portrayed in a fresco by Pintoricchio in the Piccolomini chapel the Siena's cathedral of St. Mary, and who held chivalric titles (knight of Jerusalem) and such important posts as administrator of the cathedral's finances.[56] It was Aringhieri who dealt with Benedetto and who collected the rent payments, in, however, an extremely irregular manner. The only regular payment noted was for 29 lire; later a whirlwind of payments began, so confusing that it seems Benedetto paid only when and what he could. In certain cases, as we will see in a later chapter, he paid not in cash but in lime.[57] In November 1480 Benedetto paid 40 of the 102 lire that he owed to Aringhieri "for rented land held at Vicho and Petricciolo."[58] The next year he declared himself again in default with the payment of another 10 fiorini, a debt that continued to grow in the following period, only slightly reduced by a few downpayments.[59]

Finally, in 1483, seven years after letting the estate, Aringhieri "settles every and all matters which we have had over the give and take of the rent agreement with Benedetto del Massaritia."[60] This was the moment of reckoning. Now, "since Benedetto and Lord Alberto want to make and settle the bill and to reduce it all to a single sum," the peasant found himself owing 52 lire and 11 soldi "on account of arrears in rent,"[61] including rent owed for the time between the drawing up of the contract and November 1, when Benedetto would leave the farm.[62]

Payment of arrears was not actually finalized on that day but dragged on for another three years in a flurry of small disbursements. At one point Benedetto and Aringhieri must have argued over the slow rate of payment, for they ended up in court. It was Benedetto's second court appearance, and everything suggests that a peasant rebelling against his rents was a paradigm of normal behavior. We discern Benedetto's "contractual" strength here, and how labor shortages allowed "the workers of the soil . . . to learn . . . to ignore debts and rent payments."[63] When the two contestants, following contemporary advice to resolve such disputes "by legal channels," heard the court decision, Benedetto had to pay his old debts, to the tune of 81 lire and 18 soldi, and share the legal expenses "incurred from this plaint" (another 4.5 lire). The peasant paid in full two months later, but not in cash; rather, he worked on lands administered by Aringhieri who, at last, in late February 1486, declared himself fully satisfied.[64]

Meanwhile, Benedetto actually took on *another* sharecropping contract while still involved in farming the Vico and Petriccio estates along with his Marciano farm. Unfortunately, we know nothing about this new farm, except that Martino, son of a former landlord of Galgano, owned it. The new plot was certainly close to the main Marciano lands, for Benedetto and his family farmed it alone and there is no sign of subletting. It must have been a small plot for the Massarizia family to cultivate it unaided.

Still, there was room enough to pasture large animals on it and sow wheat and lesser grains. On November 25, 1479, according to Martino, Benedetto "our sharecropper" paid 6 lire "for an ox hide sold when he flayed the beast." He in turn received 7 soldi he had fronted for Martino's share of a shoeing operation and a further 3 soldi, which he had had to pay at the gate as a toll when he took the hide to Siena to sell. A few days later Benedetto transported wheat to the landlord with other grains; he again paid the toll himself and had it subtracted "from the bigger sum which he still owes me," as Martino wrote.[65]

In 1480, after Galgano died and left his family in straitened circumstances, Benedetto obtained the release of Galgano's land from impoundment. He later bought part of this land, on which there was a "big farmhouse," from his niece Vangelista, daughter of Galgano. The cost was 100 fiorini.[66] When the sale contract was drawn up, Benedetto paid half of this sum to Angelino di Vanni, father-in-law of Vangelista, and promised to pay the other 50 fiorini to Vangelista "within a year." This latter sum was the dowry of Giovanna, Galgano's widow, as declared to the notary who drew up the contract. Now that her husband was dead, it had to return to Giovanna's family, who would treat it as an integral part of Vangelista's own dowry.[67] Benedetto did pay the sum, but in many installments and not quite "within a year."

In these years Benedetto's complex strategy of putting Marciano at the heart of his interests bore fruit. It was not simply a matter of obtaining shelter contracts nor of acquiring small plots as insurance against the possible loss of the bigger farm. His was a deliberate strategy to enlarge and improve the already vast farm purchased from the Borghesi. In May 1481 the peasant bought from master Gregory, "the doctor of arts and medicine," two bits of land bordering his big holding in Marciano for 100 fiorini.

But the seller "kept ownership until paid in full, within nine years" of this land. For his part Benedetto undertook to pay in 10-fiorini installments, but with each payment he demanded a proportional decrease of the interest the seller expected. This was 17 lire per year, about 4.25 percent.[68] In this case as before Benedetto's land transactions were not characterized by regular payments. But the indebtedness that resulted from his inability to honor his agreements punctually grew with each passing year. In 1488, seven years after signing the contract and two before the landlord could reclaim his property, Benedetto had seen his debt to the doctor grow to 115 fiorini, 15 more than had been agreed to originally.[69] It is almost as if Benedetto had been paying rent (the interest on his debt) during all those years, rather than installments on the land itself. The result was that the land was destined to return to the original owner soon, after he had enjoyed its income, while the peasant had farmed these neighboring plots with little exertion and paid a very modest fee for the right. In the end, it seems that Benedetto himself had spied an easy way to exploit lands that he was not really interested in owning.

What contributed decisively to increasing his indebtedness was, rather, the Marciano estate. In 1483 he was a long way from paying off the loan obtained from master Giusto and his brother with half the estate as security. After acquiring the eighth-share in 1479, it seems Benedetto was unable to pay anything back. Some three of the six years allotted for repayment remained, but Benedetto himself realized he would never be able to meet his obligations in that interval. He therefore asked (and the owners agreed) to "extend the established time for paying back." But there had been changes since the mortgage had been initiated; master Giusto, who drew up the contract, had died. His two brothers and heirs, Giovanni and Vittorio, agreed to the extension of another six years for repaying the 400 fiorini, but they significantly increased the burden of other terms of the contract. For example, when Benedetto wanted to pay off the debt, he had to give a year's notice and continue to pay the usual "rent" throughout that year.

More significant, the interest rate increased. The original payment of thirty-two staia of wheat (or maybe wine), about a 10-percent interest rate, changed to a "yearly payment" of fifth-two staia of "good" wheat, fifty-two of equally good wine, one staio of oil, one of broad beans and a pile of firewood. All was to be brought to the brothers' house at Benedetto's expense, whereas the 1476 contract provided for him to pay only the transportation costs, not the tolls.[70]

The cost of the cash Benedetto obtained by mortgaging his property had, in sum, considerably grown. It is difficult to translate precisely into money these payments in kind. But the interest rate was certainly more than doubled, though less than tripled. It had moved from altogether acceptable levels to progressively steeper ones as the due date for final repayment was pushed forward. By now Benedetto was paying interest of just under 30 percent, a rate below that which might give rise to accusations of public usury and actually within the bounds allowed by city governments, but still very stiff.[71]

Yet even as Benedetto sought an extension, he also purchased a vineyard with arable, woods, olives and orchards, as well as a house with a vat.[72] This estate, sold by master Giusto's same brothers, lay in Terrenzano, not far from Montalbuccio but far enough from Marciano to suggest that he had to farm this plot himself as well. Probably this was the estate on which one of his sons lived and worked. Benedetto promised to pay 95 fiorini in two installments. The first 55 were due within the next six months, and the remainder six months later, although the owners reserved for themselves the yield of the year of the sale. This transaction took place on May 13, that is, very close to the harvest, and the purchase price did not include the labor performed, and almost finished, for the owner by the preceding cultivator.[73]

One year later, a modest purchase was added to the already conspicuous property that Benedetto had built up at Marciano by delicately balancing debts and mortgages. He bought two staiori of fallow land at Marciano,[74] and although its exact position is not specified it seems likely that it was very close to the land he had already bought from the same landlord, which had boundaries in common with the estate. The issues raised by the Marciano purchase, and by its extensions and accretions, were settled only at the end of Benedetto's life. In 1488 he still declared "half a property . . . divided with Vittorio and Giovanni of Volterra, worth 325 fiorini."[75] But on October 30, 1492, the two brothers "sold" to Benedetto their "part ownership" at Marciano for the 400 fiorini loaned many years earlier.[76]

At the conclusion of his labyrinth of debts and engagements, Benedetto managed to pull out and not lose his land. His strategy had been fruitful. The purchases of small plots, the sales of marginal property, the years as a renter or sharecropper had all served to save the bigger estate. Contrary to every expectation, when Benedetto bet against urban capital, he won.

6

The Women of the Household

Life was not easy for those born female in the fifteenth century (actually, the same applies to most other centuries, too). Families lamented the birth of a daughter, rather than a son, describing it as a disaster. For urban families, daughters were mouths to feed who contributed little to the household's income. Families living on the land considered the birth of a girl as a loss of two strong arms for the heavy work required by country life: at the very most peasant girls could carry out the lighter tasks in the household economy, such as pasturing the flocks or tending the courtyard animals. But whether urban or rural, all women brought the worry of assembling a dowry to their families, unless the family could consider supporting them for their entire lives. Putting together a dowry was troubling for poor and even average families. Indeed, in fifteenth-century Sienese and Florentine tax returns there are often pleas for a lightening of the tax burden on account of the family's need to marry off, and hence provide dowries for, the girls of the house.

Preachers frequently tried to convince their audiences that the size of dowries had attained unacceptably high levels. In the very years when Benedetto del Massarizia was active, the commune of Siena legislated to control the size of dowries, claiming that families were being ruined by inflated expectations in the grooms' households. The commune claimed that a dowry of 800 fiorini, which until recently had been considered substantial, had come to be seen as miserly. Perhaps the legislators exaggerated in their grim picture when they maintained that urban fathers were forced to seek husbands for their daughters in the countryside, where dowry levels were lower, or to place their daughters in nunneries. The General Council concluded that a middling family could be financially ruined by having a single daughter to marry off. Despite their exaggeration, Siena's rulers had identified a real problem. In view of this, it is easy to understand why baby girls always outnumbered boys among the unwanted infants left in church doorways or in front of hospitals in all fifteenth-century cities.

But women were vital to the social and economic fabric of both country and city. Although they left faint traces on urban production processes, women could carry out many jobs, even those traditionally considered masculine. This was especially true when women inherited the family workshop from a dead husband, even if in their new role they took on an ambiguous gender identity. The eloquent Sienese Dominican preacher Saint Bernardino captured this ambiguity when he referred to such women as "half men." [1]

Some women actually joined guilds. This was more common in Germany and France than in Italy, but in north central Italy there are examples of female guild-members. In the waning Middle Ages such opportunities for women shrank, and women were increasingly marginalized, restricted to the work of spinning and weaving, and placed under the authority of male members of craft guilds.

Renaissance women's productive capacities were equal to men's, and they could also acquire equal experience. For example, Alessandra Mancighi Strozzi maintained the family on her own when the menfolk left Florence, exiled to Naples; and Margherita Datini managed what was perhaps Christian Europe's largest corporation when her husband Francesco traveled abroad, displaying steely nerves and business acumen equal to his. Still, women never enjoyed an autonomy comparable to that of men. In fifteenth-century Florence women could inherit property only if there were absolutely no male heirs, even from lateral branches of the family. Women's control of property was very limited. Moreover, in cities, women of the upper classes almost never participated in choosing their husbands. The choice was their families' and was based on calculations of political and economic advantage, not on the love interests of the women. But among the down-and-out no one was interested in marital alliances, and as one descends the social ladder women acquired more autonomy in marriage strategies. In the countryside there were also economic reasons for women's greater autonomy. Female peasants administered the income from running the chicken coops and other poultry operations directly, without involving their husbands.

Rural women participated in practice in the labor of farming even if they were not mentioned in contracts. They had specific tasks, working in vineyards or vegetable gardens, or (as just mentioned) tending the poultry and pasturing pigs and sheep. In sharecropping contracts women were required to fulfill the "honorary" payments to the landowner, that is, all the jobs not directly related to farming. Thus they spun wool for the landlord and did domestic chores in his house on specified days. Their life in a house at the center of the farm, the "central space" of sharecropping, enabled women to work simultaneously on the land and as mothers and administrators of households.

Quite often female peasants worked as wet nurses for city children, so as to improve the family's finances. Sometimes the baby belonged to the landlord, but sometimes it was an abandoned child, left before some urban hospital, which then assigned the infant to a peasant wet nurse who was compensated in money.[2] Often it was the husband of the wet nurse who picked up the payments and vouched for the baby's health to the hospital administrators. In such cases the peasant was registered as a "male wet nurse."

The first woman who left traces in this story is an unknown, a woman consigned to namelessness by the booklets, who married Meo on an unknown day and gave birth to Benedetto, Galgano, and perhaps another child, who also remains in the shadows of our history. She outlived Meo by more than ten years, for in 1465, old and widowed, she lived with her son Benedetto, who implored the tax office to be benevolent toward his mother in view of her old age.[3]

There is more precise information only for the second generation of women in the Massarizia family—the generation of Benedetto, Galgano, and Giovanni. These women entered the household in the twenty years between the late 1430s and the late 1450s. The first is Mariana, who married Benedetto in 1438.[4] The knowable story of her life with him is contained in two dates: 1438, when she was married, and 1459, when she is mentioned as already dead. Her name is not listed in the brief notice of the small sum spent by Benedetto "for 19 pounds, 3 ounces of wax in a pair of lanterns and 6 torches and 9 pounds of candles . . . for the burial of his wife" and "for the funeral decorations . . . when she died."[5] There is nothing else about her. She was included in the memoirs of her husband only because she predeceased him. If she had died after him, there almost certainly would not have been even this most humble homage to her memory.

But Benedetto did not remain alone for long. Because of the necessity of providing for his family, as well as for help in the fields, he took another wife—Giovanna—at an unspecified moment.[6] Before this second wedding, Giovanni and Galgano also married. In August 1446 the former arranged a contract for the dowry of Cristofana. Because his father was dead, his uncle, Meo, represented the Massarizias in the meeting with the father of the fiancée. Several years later, in 1454, Galgano married a woman named Giovanna, and in this case too—for time-honored custom required a father to entrust a woman to another father—it was the older brother, Benedetto, who took the place of the paterfamilias.[7] He appeared with Galgano before a notary who drew up the contract for the dowry.

There was clearly a tendency to seek a spouse outside one's own village, where it was difficult to meet a person not too closely related for a permissible marriage. The villages of Montalbuccio, Marciano, and Casciano were inhabited by few families, and these diminished in number as time passed. For example, Montalbuccio decreased from nine households in 1410 to only two at the end of the century, and in the first thirty years of the following century it seems that only the Massarizia family remained. The story is the same for the other two villages.

This rural depopulation made it very difficult to find a spouse near one's village. If a potential spouse did live nearby but was somehow related, canon law might prohibit marriage unless one pursued a laborious request for a special dispensation.[8] However impractical endogamy was, it was necessary to turn to the outside, expanding the concept of marriage with people "from one's same milieu" to include neighboring parishes.[9]

Still, one usually remained within the area where one could personally evaluate, without risk of surprise, the substance and assets of the prospective in-laws. Thus, Caterina, wife of Benedetto's son Mattia, came from a village that, though distant from Benedetto's lands, was quite near to the land Mattia cultivated in Monteforelli. And when Caterina remarried about a year after Mattia died, her new family lived some distance from the lands of the Massarizia but close to her family of origin, to which, following custom, she had returned upon the death of her husband.[10]

But sometimes marriages were contracted from farther away. Giovanna, wife of Galgano, came from San Martino a Strove, rather distant from the village of her husband. Similarly, Vangelista, Galgano's daughter, found a husband in another faraway place: Badia al Piano (Alfiano), southwest of Siena.[11]

Marriage placed Benedetto's daughter Bernardina among those few who succeeded in leaving the country and moving to the city, a fate usually reserved for people of a higher social status.[12] Her husband, Paolo di Giovanni Lapini, lived with his father in Siena, and "at present they are in the neighborhood of Uvile, in his house."[13] It is a pity that we cannot know the trade of this man, as his neighborhood traditionally was inhabited by woolworkers. In 1371, some decades before Bernardina's marriage, the Sienese *ciompi*, as woolworkers were called, rose in revolt against the commune and work conditions and violently shook up Siena's institutions, though, like that of their Florentine counterparts in 1378, their rebellion swiftly came to ruin.

In sum, marriage united people living relatively close to each other, who met at a market or village festival. But one knew only the essentials about the future spouse—age, social status, and in the case of women, the size of the dowry—through a marriage broker. At times, these rural unions resulted from a calculation of reciprocal advantage more than from falling in love, roughly as they did in cities.[14]

Hence, if a woman sought a husband, she looked for a man who could guarantee a decent standard of living, and if a man sought a wife, the dowry was the prime concern. The family of the wife gave money and goods to the family of the husband not as a gift, but rather as a loan to "guarantee the formation and the maintenance of a new family unit."[15] Certain objects, certain linens, certain garments comprised the dowry of a country girl, an advance on her paternal inheritance over which, from the moment of marriage, she no longer held rights.[16] If a peasant could not provide a dowry for his daughter, he asked his landlord for help, or if he had a bit of his own land, he mortgaged it and took a loan or, more simply, he bought the trousseau on credit, repaying it bit by bit, as we have seen with Giovanni.[17]

Finding the money for a dowry was not easy. Giovanni's complaints, the problems with which Vangelista wrestled, and the delayed payments to the families of the in-laws of debts contracted for the dowry must have been as common in the country as they were in cities. In a village, and even among less poor peasants, there were none of the splendid dowries by which "an only daughter could destroy a modest household," as city dwellers lamented.[18] The average value of a peasant dowry was about 200 lire, though for the country this was no small sum.

Benedetto's first wife brought a dowry of 160 lire in 1438, whereas Giovanni's wife, Cristofana, brought a higher sum in 1446: 200 lire, the standard almost unvarying value of rural dowries.[19] The dowries of Giovanna, wife of Galgano, in 1453 and many years later, in 1490, that of Brandina, wife of Meo di Benedetto, were also worth 200 lire.[20] Instead, the dowry that Caterina brought to her marriage with Mattia in 1475 was 180 lire.[21] Much smaller than the others was the dowry of Margherita, who married Francesco, another son of Benedetto, in 1465. Her share was not more than 120 lire, practically half what the other women brought to the household.[22]

Some of the dowries included objects and household goods. Certainly Massarizia girls brought such things to their husbands, though for these women, in contrast to the women who married into the family, it is difficult to establish the monetary worth of the dowry.[23] In about 1472, Iacoma, daughter of Benedetto, brought her husband a dowry with, among other things, a bed, a bedcover, and a bedstead.[24] Some years later, her sister Bernardina, took to her husband, Paolo Lapini, along with the rest of the dowry, a "hooded garment made of French-style cloth like new, . . . a bed, one bedstand like new" worth in total 62 lire.[25]

On the other hand, the dowry for Galgano's daughter Vangelista was composed of her mother Giovanna's dowry, which had been returned to Giovanna when Galgano died.[26] It fell to Benedetto to face the demands of his sister-in-law. In 1482, about a year after the death of Galgano and with Vangelista's marriage to Girolamo d'Agnolo imminent, the three parties—Benedetto, Giovanna, and the future family of Vangelista—presented themselves to the notary to make official the restoration of the 200 lire which, twenty-eight years before, had been Giovanna's dowry. The sum, as established by common agreement, would be given back within one year and would "be invested for the security of the dowry of the lady Evangelista."[27] This repayment, however, must have been delayed a bit beyond the agreed time because in 1484 Benedetto found himself paying eight ducats "as part of the payment of the large sum Benedetto owed to Girolamo as part of the dowry of lady Vangiolista his wife and niece of Benedecto."[28]

Giovanna's dowry was not the only one reimbursed by the Massarizia family. This task—the unfortunate economic corollary of mourning a deceased relative—again fell onto the shoulders of Benedetto in 1480, when he had had to return the dowry of Caterina, widow of his son Mattia. On that occasion, Benedetto paid to his daughter-in-law's two brothers, 76 lire "as a partial restitution of the dowry of Caterina." The sum was immediately given to the future husband of the widow, who three months later received the remainder.[29] Paying two restitutions, for a total of almost 100 fiorini, in scarcely two years may not have destroyed him, but there is no doubt that their combination posed a problem for Benedetto.

7

Cultivation and Animal Husbandry

 The lands worked by these peasants were generally characterized by intercultivation, or polyculture, which, in fifteenth-century Tuscany, typified the holdings of both city owners and independent peasants. The main difference between the Massarizia family's land and that which they rented or sharecropped was that fruit trees were more prevalent on the latter, in contrast to the greater importance of woodlands on their own lands.

It is not surprising to find fruit trees on the farm at Terrenzano, sharecropped for a city owner or on those rented from the abbey of San Galgano. Sienese law of the 1400s required peasants to plant four fruit trees and four olive trees a year on farms of sufficient size.[1] Fruit enjoyed favor in city markets, which drove its prices to levels almost equal to that of wheat. City owners' consequent attention to their trees frequently annoyed peasants who, if they did not actually overprune the fruit trees until they were damaged, devoted scanty attention to their care; fruit was distant from their interests.[2]

Woodland, in contrast, prevailed on peasant holdings. The Massarizia's trees were likely deciduous, perhaps oaks and other trees typical of Mediterranean scrub, as suggested by the six staiori "of forest, that is juniper thickets" on the Montalbuccio holding. Peasants needed woodland as pasture for their pigs, but also for two important activities: gathering firewood for use or sale and producing lime. Benedetto established a small trade in both of these areas.

If it is true that diet determines the entire rural economy, the marked preference for wheat bread—on city and country tables—led peasants, including the Massarizia family, to cultivate wheat in preference to other cereals.[3] In the entire Sienese countryside, the other grains made up 15 to 20 percent of the production and never exceeded 30 percent.[4] Yet it is not possible to know how much the Massarizia planted or harvested; the meager indications of the twelve staia that Benedetto sowed in the lands of the Cabella or the four or five staia at Montalbuccio do not allow a prudent hypothesis.[5]

The Massarizia family complained about the scarcity of their harvests, especially to tax officials. Among Galgano's numerous debts were 18 lire due for two staia of wheat, 20 lire owed for another two loads, and an additional 4 lire for the same reason.[6] At his death, a debt for wheat was still outstanding.[7] Giovanni, too, contracted more than one debt for wheat, one of which cost him the loss of some land. Not even Benedetto was spared the shortfalls at harvest time, although his situation was not as difficult as Galgano's. In some years, he had to buy wheat in markets at Siena and even farther away.[8]

Meadows appear to have played a marginal role. They are mentioned only once, in reference to Giovanni's property.[9] The fact that Benedetto purchased hay suggests that it was not customary to cultivate it.[10] Instead of feeding his sheep and cows with hay, he probably relied on lesser grains (like sorghum), leguminous plants, tree leaves, shoots from the vines, and the grass growing along drainage ditches.[11] Fallow lands, however, were part of the Cabella, Casciano, and Marciano properties. The landscape thus included uncultivated areas, whether these were left voluntarily wild or allotted to pasture or future cultivation.[12]

At Casciano there was also a garden. A typical characteristic of hill agriculture, a garden could be cultivated with little fertilizer.[13] Since its products were almost completely exempt from the landowner's exactions, the garden constituted a "duty-free zone of the holding." This valuable supplement to their food supply was central to the nutritional well-being of peasants.[14] Some communities, recognizing the importance of gardens, promulgated severe regulations for their protection.[15]

The territory worked by these peasants was ideal for two specialized crops: olives and grapevines.[16] Olive trees grew on the land that Benedetto sold at Casciano, and on the land at Marciano and at Terrenzano.[17] Peasants never cultivated olives alone. They grew other crops around the trees, for plowing and hoeing allowed rain to penetrate the soil and also broke the tiny fissures in the soil through which water could evaporate: working the soil around olives conserved water as well as producing food.[18]

Probably, the brush on land Benedetto bought for four moggia of lime in 1485 was destined to form rough brooms to clear the ditches around the olive trees (as well as having other uses, discussed below).[19] Equally probable, he used the remains of lime-making as precious fertilizer for his olive orchard.[20]

There is no sign of trade in olive oil, so we must presume oil was for household use only. Olives began to be important in the Sienese countryside only in the 1400s.[21] The Massarizia family were involved in this major agricultural "transformation," and, both in growing olives and in not sacrificing the trees to cereal cultivation, they resembled city owners.[22]

To produce their oil, these peasants had to borrow an animal to turn the oil press. Benedetto's son Lorenzo asked the Sienese convent of San Francesco, to which the family regularly furnished wine, for one. The friars loaned them "a horse . . . for the olive mill," charging them 4.5 lire for the privilege.[23]

The popularity of wine, together with white bread, had grown to unprecedented levels by the second half of the 1300s.[24] Tuscan city dwellers, whatever their social class, liberally consumed wine. Inhabitants of fifteenth-century Florence seem to have consumed about four-fifths of a liter per capita each day, and fourteenth-century Sienese may have consumed on average 1.15 liters per day.[25] A great variety of wines was on the market, each type having its own clientele, but the taste for wine unified very disparate social classes.[26] Those who could not afford the costliest wines that accompanied the meals of the rich could drink *acquarello* (watery wine), the habitual drink of poor peasants, whose higher-quality production went to the landlord.

The hills around Siena, with their low vineyards, often planted in mixed cultivation together with grains, were a favored site of wine production, particularly where city owners and sharecropping leases prevailed.[27] Vineyards were, in fact, the most widespread system of land improvement, the easiest way to increase land's profitability.[28] Although selling surplus wheat was extremely difficult, marketing a surplus of wine was quite easy. As Tuscan wines conquered more markets, the importance of wine to city owners' profits grew.[29] Agricultural treatises considered it "the imperative of the times: to increase wine production by planting new vines, rejuvenating and maintaining those already in existence."[30]

In the 1300s, fields were increasingly planted with grapevines. Owners showed a marked interest in improving the quality of their production: less favorable zones of open plain were abandoned, and hill planting was intensified in all areas where farm size allowed mixed cultivation.[31] Although the cost of establishing a vineyard was not excessive, it still required a high capital investment (relative to agricultural profits), and there was no return until the vines matured: the first full vintage might come some five years after planting.[32]

Landowners' strong interest in grapevines led them to divide this crop with cultivators differently from other products of the soil. It was not uncommon for renters, who paid in cash, to owe portions of their wine, or for sharecropping contracts to exclude wine from the division into halves that applied to other produce; instead, the landlord would receive either the major portion, the best quality wine, or the first pressing.[33]

Although this system favored the owner, viticulture was not always detrimental to the peasants. Work on the vines was often paid labor and thus supplemented the peasant's family budget. It was also possible to sell any surplus; although peasants rarely had extra wheat to sell, they were more likely to have some wine casks to send to the market.[34]

The Massarizia family seem to fit perfectly into this general picture. All the land that they cultivated—whether owned or not—had some vineyard. Galgano had one at Casciano, and Benedetto had a "little piece of vineyard of about five staiori" equipped "with a little building in which to make wine" and with three vats at Marciano. Giovanni possessed four staiori of vineyard near Belcaro, as well as two staiori at Montalbuccio. Benedetto's land at Terrenzano was called "vineyard"— though it actually supported mixed cultivation—and was furnished with a vat. Finally, Benedetto had a vineyard equipped with five vats on the lands acquired from the Borghesi family. Even Tommè del Massarizia, the last, impoverished family member for whom we have a written record, worked in a vineyard, paradigmatic of a family actively engaged in viticulture through generations.

Benedetto and his sons developed the sale of wine into an important business. Their clients seem to have been from all social classes; their preferred client was a landowner to whom Benedetto repeatedly sold wine and *acquarello*, though the convent of San Francesco of Siena was also a customer.[35] Benedetto even paid some of his debts with wine, which was not unusual in this area.[36] His active involvement in the wine business seems greater than the payment receipts in his two little books indicate. To judge from the frequency of tolls he paid on wine entering the city, especially in the best season for sales, "from Lent to the end of August, if the wine lasts," this family activity increased over the years. The twelve loads of wine sold in May 1503 were the last traceable witness of a business that seemed to have become not only a supplement of the family budget, as it was with Benedetto, but a major activity.[37]

Sales of Wine by Pietro

March-April 1499	8 loads = 7.3 quintali
April-June 1500	24 loads = 21.9 quintali
February-July 1501	28 loads = 25.5 quintali
February-May 1502	31 loads = 28.3 quintali
May 1502	10 loads = 9.1 quintali
May 1503	12 loads = 10.9 quintali

Sales of Wine by Benedetto

1460	17.5 loads = 15.9 quintali
1462	16 loads = 14.6 quintali
1463	15 loads = 13.7 quintali
1482	7 loads = 6.4 quintali

Judging from their tax declarations, the family had few animals. Giovanni spoke of "an ox that I have" and Benedetto declared "three beasts of burden" worth 20 fiorini in 1465, as well as an unknown number of animals present in 1481 on the lands in Marciano.[38] However, the presence of animals on all cultivated lands—especially certain animals like mules, pigs, sheep, chickens, and oxen—was a constant with rare exceptions. Yet the need for grain and other crops meant that little land could be spared for pasture, and herding large animals was very restricted.[39] Nonetheless, the three peasants must have used a considerable number of animals, especially oxen, to work their lands.

In the first period of their history, in the 1450s, the family already used a considerable "stable." In 1451 Meo paid to pasture five oxen, and the following year Benedetto paid for the right to pasture the same number of animals on common lands.[40] Sometime between 1452 and 1453, Benedetto's oxen became six, perhaps because he had acquired a calf in the meantime.[41] Since the average number of oxen used in the fields was two to four for lighter soils and six to eight for more heavy soil, the number of animals Benedetto actually used was respectable, though, of course, when he had an odd number of oxen, he may have borrowed an animal from neighbors.[42]

To house the animals, the Massarizia family used real stables, not patched-up ruins as one frequently finds in the Tuscan countryside of this period: despite the advice of that "Renaissance man" Leon Battista Alberti (who advocated building special stables, "to respond to the needs of cows and sheep, not less than to those of one's wife"), the population decline after 1348 consigned many abandoned dwellings to reuse as stables.[43] On Benedetto's land at Marciano, there were buildings that were obviously stables. And when a part of the Montalbuccio farm passed to Benedetto's cousin Giovanni, the house with its lands "and the stable" on them were named as part of the property.

One cannot know how many of the animals for whose pasture the Massarizia paid were owned by them and how many belonged to the landowner. The peasant family probably did not own them all if, as has been hypothesized, they chose plots to sharecrop in order to use the animals on the land belonging to others, but also on their own. The "remainder from the loss of oxen" settled between Benedetto and Galgano, on the one side, and Giacomo del Besso, on the other, and that "valuation of animals" with Bartolomeo Benucci may have been either part of the sharecropping contract or a pact of shared ownership.[44] The animals valued in 1474, when Benedetto's son Lorenzo rescinded the sharecropping relationship with Giovanni di Cesario and settled the "value of the oxen," certainly belonged to the landlord.[45] Likewise, when Benedetto obtained the money from "one ox hide sold when it was skinned," the animal belonged to his landlord, as did the beast of burden for which he had paid the expenses of shoeing.[46]

But the other oxen must be considered the property of the peasants, who bought new animals with some frequency, as soon as the old ones wore out in the fields. The recurrent acquisition of young oxen "for replacement" is proof that intentionally breeding animals was rare.[47] A young ox was acquired in 1450, another two in 1452, and two more were in shared ownership between the end of that year and the beginning of the next.[48] Although an ox had been bought in 1475, the following year Benedetto wrote that "Benedetto di Cristofano Palmieri of Prata in Maremma exchanged with us one young ox for an old ox and he gave us a young ox." He got 21 lire in exchange, since "we agreed that we owed him 21 lire in addition for the young ox," paid partly in money ("two broad ducats") and partly in kind ("3 lire and 2 soldi which he got in shoes from Simone di Stefano").[49] In thirty-five years, all told, if the two books included all the transactions, Benedetto made ten new acquisitions. This rate of replacement (one every three and a half years) indicates an early and marked wearing out of the animals.[50]

One cannot know if the number of animals used was proportionate to the extent of the peasant's lands. Nor can one guess at the expenses of maintaining the stable because the written figures next to the animal transactions are often only downpayments. Furthermore, the animals' feeding costs escape us entirely. One can observe only that in every exchange of animals this peasant paid from 20 to 50 lire, according to the condition and the age of the animal.

In addition, peasants paid for the right to pasture. These recurring payments average about a lira and a half for each animal brought to pasture. Some of the animals were held in *soccida*, the type of shared-ownership contract that, on one hand, benefited the peasant, giving him manure, food, cheese, and wool,[51] and, on the other hand, permitted the city owners to obtain high profits from investments, as any risk of devaluing the initial outlay was practically absent.[52]

Payments for the Pasturage of Oxen

Year	Number of Animals	Amount Paid	Page in Booklet
1451	5	7 lire, 6 sol.	A 1
1452	5	7 lire, 10 sol.	A 2v
1452	6	9 lire	A 6
1454	?	7 lire, 8 den.[a]	A 7v
1460	?	16 lire[a]	A 13v
1465	4	6 lire	A 12v
1476	?	3 lire	A 18v

[a] The payment includes that paid for the right to collect wood.

In contrast to the obligation, current in fifteenth-century sharecropping contracts, for peasants to pay for their work animals on their own, for smaller animals landlords were willing to split costs. Benedetto and Galgano had young oxen and sheep in shared ownership; these animals would not wear out and depreciate, as did mature working animals, but would increase in value, becoming attractive investments for urban landlords. It is difficult to identify the social class of the "partners," as we know only two: an artisan (a cloth cutter) and a school teacher. But they fit the pattern established in other areas, in which it was not wealthy owners, but rather well-off people of moderate means who tended to engage in this type of investment.[53] In contrast, they were forced to buy work animals themselves, even as sharecroppers.[54]

In 1454 Benedetto had a contract of *soccida* for two young oxen with the cloth cutter Antonio di ser Bartolomeo. Between winter of that year and the following spring, Benedetto paid him 65 lire that "he owes to the association for animals."[55] We do not know which of the two possible contract arrangements—half of profits and half of losses, or all profits and all losses—was adopted in this case. (The "half of profits and half of losses" clause obliged peasants to invest half the capital—which actually the landowners paid in advance—and to absorb half of any losses or gains over the initial outlay. If the peasant could not repay the capital his landlord advanced for him, he paid with his share of the animal. With "all profits and all losses" contracts, peasants had to pay the entire value of the animal's original worth at contract's end; thus they owned all the animal, risking everything if it died but gaining everything if its value increased.)[56]

Benedetto also had part ownership of sheep with Bartolomeo di Vitale, a Sienese school teacher. In 1465 Benedetto paid him 4 lire "for two wools of the sheep held from me, which Benedecto sold at my orders," as Bartolomeo wrote. The contract was dissolved in 1468 when "I, master Bartolomeo, call myself satisfied also of all the rest of the sheep which in any way have been held from me."[57] And although we do not know the number of sheep or the nature of the contract, it is worth noting that the flock was an indispensable element of a farm for the wool and the food it provided.[58]

Pigs, too, were typical of Sienese rural life.[59] They had a primary role in the country economy, though less so than in the early medieval period when the sylvo-pastoral sector was most prominent.[60] Held outright or in *soccida*, pigs were common and most peasants were swineherds during certain periods of the year, enough so that rural communities legislated against indiscriminate pasturage of these animals, thought to damage agriculture.[61] Pigs were kept in the forests, in contact with boars with whom they interbred and shared such characteristics as leanness and long legs.[62] Since no part of the animal was wasted, pigs played an important role in the medieval diet, especially because their meat could be preserved all year. The task of preserving pig meat actually brought the citizens of Carpentras, France, together in "associations for salting pork" in the 1400s, and specialists of this trade formed a guild in late medieval Bologna.[63] Benedetto bought pigs frequently.

Their cost ranged from about 6 lire to around 8, depending on weight, although in 1482 he bought a pig that cost twice as much as the others. Chickens completed the farmyard collection, judging from their presence in the division of produce between Benedetto and the owner of the land he sharecropped.[64] But far more than chickens, it was beasts of burden that had the far greatest importance. Commerce in wine, wood, and lime would have been almost impossible without them. Benedetto bought the first of them, a horse costing 20 lire in 1465, from the nuns of the monastery of Ognissanti through the schoolmaster with whom he had a contract of shared ownership. The teacher advanced the sum and it was repaid four months later "in several installments."[65] Some years later, Benedetto's son Pietro acquired a mule, a sought-after animal, for a decidedly high sum: 16 fiorini, more than three times the cost of the horse. Generally these tough and versatile animals were too expensive for peasants.[66] This, too, was a "deferred-payment" purchase; the settlement of 1473—our only notice of this mule—refers to the transaction occurring "already a long time ago."[67] A few years later, Benedetto acquired a second mule for an approximately equal amount: 63 lire and 16 soldi also paid a bit at a time.[68]

To create, maintain, renew, or strengthen his stock of animals, Benedetto scoured the countryside near and far. Buying livestock required searches over sometimes long distances, in the markets of the region or, more modestly, in the cottages of other peasants.[69] In addition to the obvious contacts with the owners and merchants of the nearest city center, Benedetto did business as far away as Badia a Isola, the remotest outpost of the Sienese territory, and even farther, in Florence's countryside.[70]

8

The Lime Kiln

 The peasant who took firewood to sell in the city on the back of his donkey is such a familiar image that Ambrogio Lorenzetti included it as a typical scene in his well-known fresco *The Effects of Good Government*. The medieval city was a large consumer of firewood, for both basic needs like heating and specialized ones on building sites and in industry. The latter, including ceramics kilns, glassworks, and metal-working factories, all required wood from the countryside and encouraged a significant wood market.[1] The rural population responded with a veritable attack on the woodlands, which reached worrisome dimensions in Tuscany by the mid-1500s.[2]

The Massarizia family, in addition to their wine business, also traded in wood. This activity does not emerge from the two little books, which record only a sale of twenty loads.[3] Rather, it can be seen indirectly in

Donkeys carrying their loads inside the city wall of Siena. Those at bottom left are carrying firewood. Detail from Ambrogio Lorenzetti's *Effects of Good Government*. Palazzo Pubblico

the records of the tolls due at the gates of the city or the exaction owed for cutting wood in the common woodlands.[4] On several occasions, Benedetto and Galgano paid for the right to cut wood in the Selva del Lago; in 1452, 55 lire and 16 soldi were exacted "for the tax allotment on wood, dead wood and straw taken from the Selva." In 1454, they paid another 7 lire and 8 denari for a tax "on oxen and for the tax on dead wood," that is, of firewood obtained not from cutting down trees but from gathering dry branches. At least once the brothers had to take out loans to make these payments.

Benedetto's acquisition of "a forest, that is of wood" seems linked to this trade in wood. He bought this tract in Villanuova for 16 lire from a city owner.[5] It must have been to unload this wood that he rented a warehouse in Siena. But although some of the wood went to the city, a good part was used in Benedetto's other flourishing commercial activity: making and selling lime.

Any community needs lime kilns able to produce abundant lime for all sorts of building work. Various guilds associated with the construction industry included the obligation to produce raw materials, including lime, in the statutes regulating the activities of all members. For example, in 1441 the masons' guild (Arte della Pietra) of Siena required by statute that the guild operate a kiln to produce lime, chalk, and bricks. This was supposed to guarantee a regular supply for all construction sites in the city while also preventing the speculation of private producers by marketing materials at a controlled price.[6]

Early medieval buildings were held together by mortar of poor quality, but after the twelfth century mortar improved steadily in quality. After the High Middle Ages it was common to turn to quite distant kilns to obtain ingredients such as lime for mortar of high quality. This happened frequently in the construction sites of early modern Europe, from Edinburgh to Florence.

To produce lime one may use stone either from a quarry or from river beds. Quarried stone is considered better, for it takes half as much of the lime it produces to make good mortar as does lime from river stones, and for the same amount of labor. Several lubricant ingredients can be added to lime to make the mortar waterproof. In the mid-1300s the builders of the castle of Montefiascone in northern Latium added animal fats or olive oil, or even wax and resin to their lime.

The best lime comes from kilns with a complex structure, able to produce bricks as well as the lime itself. Often these two activities were undertaken in the same plant, and sometimes the guilds required that the same kiln produce both lime and bricks. But naturally enough, there were many kilns that operated for a small market niche, whose product was destined to local consumers alone. Numerous lime-makers and kiln operators had no specific, professional competence and improvised their craft. The activities of Benedetto del Massarizia were certainly of this type.

It was not difficult for lime-makers to find buyers at the many construction sites that had transformed the city of Siena in the late Middle Ages. Although the building surge in Siena had slowed by the late 1400s, the peasant lime-maker found a market in the continuing urban need for repair, renovation, and modernization of city houses.[7]

Benedetto's lime kiln probably was little more than a hole in the ground. An illustration in the 1540 Venetian edition of the Sienese engineering treatise by Vannoccio Biringuccio shows just such a hole lined with stone and equipped below with a feeder, from which "one must feed the fire with good wood and dry salt for seven or eight days according to the amount of stone fed and the season, and also according to the quality and quantity of the wood."[8] Making lime was a "skill known to educated men, but also to coarse ones," so even a peasant accustomed to working the fields could, without much difficulty, take on this challenge.[9]

It is impossible to know where Benedetto's kiln was located. Neither his books nor his declaration of income mention it. It probably was close to the house, left over from the time when the residence was built and the kiln was dug to make its bricks and lime.[10]

Benedetto paid an annual tax on his activities as a lime-maker, although one cannot quantify it because of the gaps in his books. Neither can one know the size of his business. Although the record of sales in the two books is extremely irregular, lime-making seems to have been a continuous activity that occupied a significant part of Benedetto's life. The first note of it dates to 1451, at the beginning of the two account books, and involves Benedetto's father Meo. The last annotation was made by his son Pietro. This activity was handed down from father to son and exceeds the chronological bounds imposed on this story by the beginning and ending dates of the books.

The first record of a lime sale dates to 1461. The next sale is recorded in 1471. In 1473, six moggia and one load of lime was "given in several installments" to Antonio and Giovanni di Cesario, who paid Benedetto 12 lire and 10 soldi.[11] Many years passed before another such notation, not because so much time elapsed between sales, since there were continuous taxes paid for this activity, but probably because Benedetto noted only some of these transactions in his books, perhaps the larger sales or those with deferred payments. The books record a sale of lime after Benedetto was dead and the booklets were far less meticulously updated; as in other activities, his son Pietro carried on his business. Between 1498 and 1499, in fact, Pietro was described as a "lime-maker," and he sold a fair amount of lime to the Sienese confraternity of San Girolamo.[12]

Just as with wine, lime was a means of barter for the family, a way to repay accumulated debts. Benedetto paid a shoemaker's bill in money, wine, and lime, as well as the rent on the land owned by the church of the Magione.[13] In 1481 he paid, in addition to 6 lire in money, three moggia of lime as the equivalent of the remaining 12 lire owed.[14] Similarly, the following year, he paid a part of the rent in "a cartload of bricks and lime . . . for the church of San Bartolomeo." The prior of San Martino, who in 1458 loaned Benedetto fully 101 lire and 5 soldi with which to pay some taxes, was reimbursed in lime, probably to maintain his church. The prior wrote, "for this money I had lime until 1459" and "7 loads of lime still remains to be paid" in 1461. The debt was repaid at the end of that year, when "on December 12, 1461, I had seven loads of lime from Betto and was satisfied with the payment."[15]

Cristofano di Fortunato, a woolworker, was repaid in the same way for a loan that enabled the Massarizia to buy a bed. Benedetto wrote, "For this advance, I owe him high-quality lime for all the next month of May, in the amount of 30 lire, 5 soldi, on lime worth 10 soldi per load, brought to his house in Siena." In addition, he promised to pay another 12 lire and 3 soldi to him "for 13.5 arm's-lengths of Romagna-style cloth." [16] It almost seems that these people habitually paid for things in goods rather than money. Benedetto also bought from a carpenter a bedroom chest and a bedframe, worth 22 lire and paid in lime rather than coins. "And of this money"—wrote the woodworker in Benedetto's book—"I must receive lime costing the amount of the goods sold, which lime would be worth 10 soldi per load, and it must be delivered to me by next May. . . . And if he fails to bring it to me within that time, I am not obligated to accept it." [17]

Benedetto could not have developed this trade independently of the guild association that controlled it. In 1471 the treasurer of the guild of stoneworkers, to which the lime-makers belonged at that time, received 1 lira, 18 soldi and 4 denari from Benedetto—again "in lime and in money." [18] It must have been a tax paid to exercise the trade, although the relevant records from the Sienese guilds have not survived.

Benedetto's payment to the heirs of Pietro Benassai in 1485 illustrates an interesting practice. Benedetto had bought a heath from them and paid four moggia of lime followed by two more later. A portion of this payment, "by order of me, Benassai," was not delivered to the creditor's house, but rather to the construction site of the church of the Madonna di Fontegiusta in Siena. This donation of building material as alms to the construction sites of churches, convents, or hospitals was not uncommon behavior among all social classes. Benedetto himself, some years before, had done the same thing, taking lime to the "caretakers of the Madonna di Fonte Giusta," as Antonio di Sano Umidi, one of this Madonna's caretakers, wrote in his booklet. This gesture of munificence linked his mentality with those of the more wealthy merchants and aristocrats and made him a participant in a devotion that transcended all class distinctions. [19]

9

A Family Confronts the State

In the medieval countryside, the state tax office was an agent of fear.[1] Anxiety over fiscal pressure, whether imposed by the local community or by the dominant government, weighed constantly on the peasants.[2] At times, an excessive fiscal burden could push an entire village into crisis and induce the peasants to abandon their land and seek respite in the city. In 1434 the villagers of Monteriggioni protested to Siena that their taxes remained unchanged from the time when the village was populous and "the inhabitants were rich and well off, and most owned their own land, for few urban folks meddled here," whereas now there were only some thirty inhabitants "all obliged to buy their own bread [that is, they did not produce it themselves] for now the city folk own all the land."[3] Even when peasants were not forced to flee their land, the many direct or indirect taxes rendered their lives arduous, especially when cities de-

liberately increased rural fiscal subjection (as Siena did in its hinterland during the fifteenth century). Nor were excessive taxes and compulsory loans the only problems: rural communities had to pay for the salaries of the officials appointed by cities to govern them.[4]

Because of how they operated, we cannot tell exactly how much money medieval tax bureaus took from each taxpayer. For city people, who had to pay direct taxes as individuals, some estimates of tax burdens are possible: from the fifteenth century Florence, using its *Catasto*, and then Siena, with its *Lira*, compelled everyone living within the city walls to declare in writing the annual income of each member of the household. But for the countryside such precise knowledge is beyond our reach.

The rural communities in the *contado* of a city lived under a totally different tax law. Siena determined how much each village had to pay and left the burden of dividing up the tax among the villagers to the villagers themselves. Thus, even when we know exactly how much a community was required to pay, in order to calculate the relative burden of taxation on each villager we also need to know exactly how many men were expected to contribute and their exact wealth. Usually this is not possible.

We must make do with far vaguer indicators. We can tell that tax pressure on the Sienese contado increased after 1400 and continued to grow despite the economic slump of the period and the attendant emptying of the countryside, which caused an agricultural crisis in the later fifteenth century. This suggests that Siena was more oppressive to its rural populations than was contemporary Florence. In the Florentine contado, to be sure, taxes were such that rural communities did their utmost to escape them, beginning with the taxes imposed by the *Catasto* of 1427–29; and certainly the dominant city surrendered few of its prerogatives—granting very few exemptions. But it is also certain that as the Florentine countryside grew poorer during the 1400s rural people came to be expected to pay less taxes.

Siena's rural subjects were, however, oppressed to different degrees. Our image of the downtrodden peasant sucked dry by the urban tax collectors is somewhat inaccurate. When it came to taxes, some peasants were "more equal" than others. In particular, special treatment was reserved for sharecroppers, for urban people looked upon them more magnanimously than they did upon other rustics. By lightening the tax load on sharecroppers, urban people, who almost always owned the land on which the sharecroppers toiled, were serving their own interest. Taxing sharecroppers harshly would only drive them off the land in search of areas, like nearby Florence, where conditions were better. Obviously this would drain Siena's farmlands of needed labor.

It was far wiser to keep taxes on sharecroppers light while instead increasing the burden on rural communities. It was also wiser to support sharecroppers in their disputes with the other villagers. Every time urban courts were called upon to judge, they took sides with the sharecropper against village officials or other villagers. For example, in 1436, when Siena updated rural tax assessments, the city's legislators were flooded with appeals from fellow citizens. The appeals claimed that recent wars, famines, and epidemics were excellent reasons to decrease the fiscal burden of sharecroppers alone. Instead, when rural communities tried to compel sharecroppers to participate in common services and work or pay certain tolls, or when they sought to limit sharecroppers access to village woods and pastures, Siena rose in defense of the "wronged" sharecroppers, and denounced these efforts as *malizie* (dirty tricks) of the peasantry designed to harm urban landowners.

For the most part, sharecroppers enjoyed a privileged position. Sometimes they lived in houses they owned rather than on the sharecropped farm; sometimes they could claim two residences, one in the village and one on the farm; sometimes they worked outside the village territory in which they lived; and often their dwellings were far from any administrative center. In each of these cases, sharecroppers had more and better opportunities than other rustics to escape the tax collectors. Moreover, whenever a sharecropper was also a smallholder, owning his own land, he had benefits beyond the lighter taxes. He could use on his own land the wine casks, tools, work animals, and so on of the sharecropped farm (paid for in part by the owner). He could also use the loans and cash advances the landowner gave him to help the sharecropped farm through difficult times as capital to invest on his own property.

Yet for someone like Benedetto, quite prominent in the community, the advantages of the sharecropper's status were fewer. To own a small plot next to the land one worked for an urban landlord was one thing, but to own some real wealth, however modest, as the Massarizia family eventually did, was quite another. For a family like the Massarizias the chances of getting away with tax evasion were far slighter than they were for one of their impoverished neighbors.

Benedetto's fiscal burden was heavy since his family owned more goods than others did. In addition to the direct taxes, the family weathered a deluge of indirect taxes because of its many activities. For example, the tax for pasturing animals increased with the number of animals, at an average cost of 1.5 lire per head. The right to gather wood in the communal reserve was even more expensive; at various times, Benedetto paid 22, 23, and even 55 lire, which was the value of an ox. These figures demonstrate that "profitable" supplementary activities could be costly to peasants. The tax on lime-making was particularly heavy: 10 to 30 lire was due on the kiln, an amount equivalent to the cost of a horse. Wine-making was also taxed mercilessly. For every quintal of wine that passed through the city gate, Benedetto left almost 7 soldi on the customs table.

At times, the levies were so great that peasants sought loans to keep up with them. In 1461, the prior of the Sienese convent of San Martino offered to help Benedetto and Galgano with their debt of more than 100 soldi, which dated from 1458, allowing them to repay him later, a bit at a time.[5] The fiscal policy of the state hit hardest those classes it could squeeze most easily. If peasants were even a bit enterprising, these policies suffocated their activities. The result was to repress all dynamism in a rural economy rooted in century-old productive systems.

The state also wanted its due when it registered any contract. With each marriage, the Sienese tax office required about 1.5 percent of the dowry of the bride. The percentage paid to register contracts recording the sale of land was even higher: about 3.3 percent of the declared value.

But this tax on farmland was only the beginning. Benedetto was subject to other payments on the lands he farmed, whether they were his own or sharecropped. For example, he always had to pay the tithe to the local parish church. But the only land tax that can be precisely determined is that paid each year to the city on August 15. This was the date of the Palio, a state festival that barely masked the overt reaffirmation of Siena's political and administrative domination of its subject lands. Thus, in 1452 Benedetto paid the mayor of the commune of Casciano 5 soldi "as the annual dues, for the Palio festival, on account of their property at Casciano."[6] Things did not change in the following years, although the records usually are concealed among the numerous payments for which the total of—but not the reason for—the taxation is indicated.

Ordinary taxes were not all that could be extracted. When Siena urgently needed money—and this happened with chronic frequency—officials had only to open the tax assessment registers. Since they controlled the assessment of taxable wealth, or lira, they were able to demand, on that basis, a forced loan to the state. Some loans were imposed on all payers, but others involved only certain social groups.[7] The taxed communities divided the burden among their inhabitants, who, in theory, were supposed to be reimbursed within four years.[8]

A loan was not necessarily a disaster. At repayment, interest (which could be 10 percent per year or more)[9] was owed as compensation. Restitution could be slow,[10] but in other cases it proceeded with regularity.[11] But when the public debt was transformed into a true consolidated debt,[12] the recurring frequency of such forced loans was a hardship for those of modest means, who had to immobilize their liquid assets for an indefinite period.[13] For those with some money, but not a lot like the peasants of Marciano, every loan could be, if not a catastrophe, certainly a serious inconvenience.

Benedetto's two books frequently indicate the sums paid to forced loan collectors. The presta of 1453 for the war against the count of Pitigliano[14] cost him 26 lire and 16 soldi, paid in four installments.[15] But the one the following year was still more expensive. From January to April, in monthly installments, Meo paid the collectors four times at 4 lire each time,[16] and in September he paid another 5 fiorini, for a total of a little less than 40 lire. This was the equivalent of one-fifth of the dowry that, scarcely a year before, Galgano's wife had brought.

We can follow these payments more easily through the fiscal registers than through Benedetto's notebooks. At one point, the family as a whole had to pay an extremely large amount for the "grain loan": 402 lire and 9 soldi—a small fortune. In 1474, the family paid 555 lire, 19 soldi, and 2 denari, divided into three parts of 185 lire, 6 soldi, and 4 denari that each branch of the family paid in small installments. Galgano's branch of the family could not keep up with this bloodletting, fell into default to the commune, and had its belongings repossessed.

This affair was hardly concluded, when another loan was due for "the impending war." At the beginning of 1481, state funds were low after a war in which the Papal League, the king of Naples, and the Genoese republic allied themselves against Florence and the duke of Milan. The Sienese republic had immediately and enthusiastically joined the former alliance, seeking any excuse to humiliate its old enemy. The armies of the two hosts had crossed the Val d' Elsa, ravaging it, and at Poggio Imperiale the troops of the League inflicted on the Florentines a bloody defeat "for which there was no small celebration at Siena."[17] But after peace returned, the Sienese victory was sacrificed to the renewed concord between the powerful king of Naples and the equally powerful Florentine lord Lorenzo de' Medici. The Sienese state resorted once more to a forced loan to recover from its exertions.

These communal visions of glory cost Benedetto's family 191 lire, 10 soldi, and 4 denari, and it was about the same for the other branches of the family. Although he was reimbursed for these loans (and other earlier ones) in 1485, in 1483 there had been yet another forced loan, and on 550 lire of taxable worth he paid an unknown, but surely not negligible, amount. An installment of this 1483 loan, 17 lire and 12 soldi,[18] equalled Benedetto's payment in 1495 on the loan imposed for "grain given to the king of France"[19] when Charles VIII "arrived in Siena where with the greatest hardship for the city he was lodged with all his people in the houses of the prominent citizens."[20]

In 1497 the conflict with Florence for lordship of Montepulciano again led Siena to impose another forced loan. There remain traces of the installments paid by Giovanni. The repayment came due in four years, in 1502, when his credit was 280 lire. This was restored to him in three parts, one for each son, of 93 lire, 8 soldi, and 2 denari each, reimbursed 2 or 3 lire at a time by the commune of Siena.[21]

In 1498 Benedetto's credit with the state was 619 lire and 11 soldi, but who knows for which earlier forced loans, never reimbursed, this high sum was due.[22] It was a decidedly large figure for the family, especially as the 5 percent interest probably did not repay them for the involuntary cash advance.

And the story is repeated later, with the heirs of the three heads of family. Their burden was less only because their taxable worth was smaller. They paid the state forced loans in 1500, 1502, 1509, 1526, and 1528,[23] probably without even understanding the rationale for the loans, those "reasons of the state" that were part of the "great history" of their republic. This history involved them only to the extent that it devastated their fields or made them pay taxes. The exploit of Montepulciano, the war against Florence and Milan, and what on earth was the king of France doing in Italy, Tuscany, Siena? This perhaps they did not know, but one thing they knew for certain: whatever else was his purpose, he had come to Italy to take their money. And thus it had been for ages.

10

Exit from History

By the beginning of the 1500s, the heads of the family's three branches had died. Benedetto, whose fortunes had continuously declined in his old age, was the last; he died a bit before 1502. His tax declaration in 1465 listed a small debt of 25 fiorini,[1] but later ones indicate increasingly serious debt, to pay for purchases, animals used for labor, or land added to his patrimony.[2] He always needed cash to repay the debts and loans that pepper the pages of his books. Benedetto even raised money by pawning household objects: "I find myself owing the Pietà 5 fiorini," he declared, referring to Siena's pious pawn shop, and since the Monte di Pietà evidently did not offer enough, he noted "and in addition I owe the Jew 4 fiorini."[3]

After the deaths of Benedetto, Galgano, and Giovanni, their sons remained: Pietro, Lorenzo, Francesco, and other children of Benedetto of whom we know nothing; the sons of Galgano, scarcely visible and unknown by name; and Bernardo, Antonio, and Meo who, with their many sisters, constitute the last offspring of Giovanni's line. They are all but invisible. Francesco paid the taxes on the farm at Monteforelli[4] and in 1465 was engaged to Margherita da Viteccio,[5] but how and where did his life unfold? Lorenzo worked as a sharecropper,[6] but where and with what fate? Pietro continued the trade of winemaker begun by his father,[7] and for a while he added to Benedetto's book of accounts, but he soon gave up. And if something more is known of Vangelista and her husband, it is only because their affairs were briefly intermingled with Benedetto's. Then they too disappear into the anonymity of the people without history.

How many children did Giovanna di Nanni have with her husband Sano di Giovanni da Tegoia? And did her brother succeed in paying the entire dowry to her father-in-law?[8] How did Bernardo and Antonio and his wife Lucia, and Meo and his wife Brandina, and the other unknown children of Giovanni and of Galgano live? What did they do? What did they hope for and fear in their lives, which lack even the ephemeral resurrection of the dead that documents confer?

Silence falls on their lives, their undertakings. The fiscal documents tell us about their minimal worth, scarcely above wretched poverty. Like so many smallholders, inheritance left them a tiny plot of land, scarcely supporting their livelihood.[9] Their histories are lost in the anonymity that nearly always swallows up peasants. When they discovered "wealth," they also discovered the techniques for giving an account of it; when wealth vanished, their engagement with pen and paper became useless.[10]

The last record of these people is a formal account of a brawl involving Tommè del Massarizia, of whom we are otherwise ignorant. In 1539 a question of dowries and of other usurped goods opposed him to a certain Margherita, and he tried to resolve the disagreement with the lady in short order. "On the day of Saint Michael"—wrote the notary who was at the site of the incident—"two years ago, Tommè Massaritia went in the vineyard of the lady Margarita and said forcefully to her: 'Who said that you could come here and harvest grapes in my vineyard?' And he tore the grapes out of her lap and threw them on to the ground. Then he took out a small knife and cut off her finger, and had it been a little bigger he would have cut off her hand. Then he grabbed her by the arms, yanking her, and said 'If I had a post, I'd gouge you with it.'" We do not know what happened afterward to the brutal Tommè del Massarizia. Perhaps he was condemned for violence "with the spilling of blood," or perhaps Margherita found a way to resolve the incident. Whatever happened, no notice is left of it.[11]

The last signs of this family are from 1580, when the population census recorded in Marciano "the farm of Gianni Masariti" with two men, a woman, and two children; and in Casciano, "Meio Masseritii, sharecropper of the monks of Belriguardo" with three men, one woman, and three children.[12] Whose descendants are they? Perhaps Gianni belonged to Benedetto's branch, still clinging to the status of smallholders in Marciano. And the other may have been from Giovanni's or Galgano's line, unluckier, having descended to the level of sharecroppers. It does not matter, though, for now we are dealing with empty names behind which there is no history—visible to our eyes, at least. A story that began with a Giovanni and a Meo is concluded also with a Giovanni and a Meo: a curious cycle. But in contrast to what happened to their fathers and grandfathers, no ear would hear the gurgling of their empty stomachs or the voice of their hunger, and they would be lowered to decay in the soil, just like leaves, without leaving any history.

Appendix

The Peasants' Memoir

The two booklets of Meo and Benedetto del Massarizia are kept in the Archivio della Società di Esecutori di Pie Disposizioni in Siena, marked with the numbers 311 and 312. They are paper booklets about eleven by fourteen centimeters, bound in parchment. I have assigned the letter A to the booklet containing writings produced between 1450 and 1502, and the letter B to the booklet that covers 1461 to 1485 and contains a retroactively dated document of 1439 (on pages 60–60 verso).

Booklet A, offered below, has 94 sheets, written on both sides, although sheet 27 is blank, as are the sheets between 27 and 88 verso, 90 to 93, and sheet 94. In the margins of sheets 24–24 verso, 25–25 verso, and 27 verso is the wax seal of the official who recorded the transactions. The booklet's cover is made out of a notarial document of the same period, only a few lines of which are still legible—too few to make it possible to reconstruct its provenance. On the cover, a contemporary hand wrote, "Book of Meio di Betto and Benedetto his son. 1450 to 1489" and below, faded and almost illegible, "1450." To the opening page is attached a small sheet with a scrawl, perhaps of the eighteenth century: "Two booklets covered with parchment, memoirs of Betto di Meio— Receipts of 1450 and 1460. Perhaps the owner of Montalbuccio."

Document B is made up of 64 sheets, written on both sides, of which 9 verso, 37, 59–59 verso, 61 verso, and 64 are blank. Sheets 53–64 verso are written backward as if the booklet had been used beginning on both ends: on the tops of sheets 55–64 verso there is actually a separate page numbering, from 1 to 10 beginning with the last sheet. Sheets 60–60 verso and 61, instead, were written on in the correct order, although the page numbering proceeds as described. On the cover a contemporary hand wrote the date "1461" followed by columns of paired numbers: "17, 18, 1, 18." Beneath this are two wholly illegible faded lines of writing, and further down, the name "Amb[rogi]o Spann[ ]o" is legible.

My transcription of the document does not pretend to be a full paleographic transcription. The more obvious abbreviations are reconstituted without any distinctive markings, but some common ones have been left in the text. Repetitions like fe/febbraio have been omitted. All dates, which in Siena were marked "from the Incarnation of the Lord," have been converted into modern terms. Inconsistencies in numerical notation have been retained to give the reader the full flavor of the different hands that wrote in this booklet over many years.

In spite of my best efforts, it has proved totally impossible to learn how, when, and why these booklets entered the Archivio della Società di Esecutori di Pie Disposizioni. The small sheet added to booklet A leads one to imagine an early date for its acquisition.

Booklet A

(Page 1) + 1450. On the 6th of March, Meio di Betto from Montealbuccio paid to us, Francesco and Tomaso Luti, 7 lire, 10 soldi for pasturing five oxen in the year 1450.   L 7 s 10

(Page 1v) Today, May 20th, I Chompanio di Teio received thirty lire for a young heifer I sold, and I am satisfied and fully paid; which money we got from Beto del Masaritia.   L 30

(Page 2) 1451. On this day, December 4th, I, Ghuccio di Pietro di Iacomo received six lire, 12 soldi, 6 denari from Benedetto di Meio di Betto, of Montalbuccio, as payment for money the aforesaid Meio owed me, which he had got from us a long time ago. And I declare myself fully paid for all dealings I have had with him up to today.

(Page 2v) A memoir of how on the 18th of March 1451 Betto di Meio

di Betto of Montalbuccio paid 55 lire, 16 soldi as taxes for the piles of wood and dead wood and hay he took from the Selva in this year, to me Lorenzo di Filipo, official of the 24th, as is recorded in the woodland register on page 11 and on page 122: 55 lire, 16 soldi. In addition he paid me, Lorenzo, seven lire, ten soldi as a downpayment for 5 oxen, recorded on page 84.   L 7 s 10

(Page 3) + Christ 1452. Pietro and Gionta di Iachomo di Gionta must have thirty-eight lire on June 8th, which are for a heifer he had from mine.   L 38
And they got on this day thirty-eight lire in cash, and Betto [gave] cash to Pietro.   L 38

(Page 3v) + Christ, mcccclii. Biagio di Guido Tholomei must have twenty-four lire, ten soldi, which are for a heifer I bought from Ghino di Lenzo, his sharecropper at Badia Ymola, which I got on June 11th.
                                                                                                                    L 24 s 10

(Page 4) + 1452. I, Pietro di Pauolo, mayor of Casciano, declare I received from Benetto di Meio, as the annual tax for the Palio festival, on account of their property at Casciano, five soldi.   L 0 s 5
I, Michele d'Antonio, mayor of Casciano, admit I received 5 s, 4 d from Benedetto di Meio as his share of the Palio celebrations for 1453.
                                                                                                                    L 0 s 5 d 4

(Page 4v) On the 20th day of September, 1452, Betto di Meio di Betto paid twenty lire in cash to Lorenzo di Filipo, official of the 24th. For his lime kiln for 1451. They are recorded in an entry on page 129.   L 20

(Page 5) 1452. On the 22nd of October I, friar Tomasso di Lottino, admit I received eight lire, 10 soldi in cash from Benedetto di Meio di Betto, paid by him into my own hand as rent for the house in the neighborhood of Laterino, for which he owes, by common consent, twelve lire per year. He has had it for eight and a half months, that is, he began paying on the 29th day of September 1452. On the feast of St. Michael he returned the key.   L 8 s 10
On the 28th of September 1454, I, Tomaxo di Giovanni Franci, received five fiorini, which were granted to me by Meio di Beto called Mas-

sarizia on account of his loan from Mariano Tomaxi, treasury official.

(Page 5v) + 1452. Benedetto di Meo di Betto of Montalbuccio must give thirty-two lire as rent for the lands we possess at Laterino and for all the trees, that is, for their fruits and the vineyard, with our half of the wine reserved, to be brought to Siena in his vehicle with us paying the toll, as proved by a writ of my own hand which he holds, including all houses and cellars in this rent. L xxxii

There are records on page 6.[1]

He has given as downpayment for several items in this house and farm 19 lire, twelve soldi, as revealed in his document, written by my own hand on January 17th 1452. L xviiii s xii

(Page 6) 1452. Betto di Meio di Betto from Montalbuccio paid nine lire for the pasturage of six oxen to me, Francesco di Lippo from Urbino, for 1452. L 9

On the x day of March, Betto di Meio di Betto paid fourteen lire to us, Gheri Bolghanii, as shown in the calculations on page 76. L 14

On the 14th day of July, we, Gheri Bolghanii and associates, received seventeen lire and 0 soldi, entered on page 76 in the book of calculations, which Betto paid. L 17

(Page 6v) + 1453. On the xxiiii day of November Meo di Betto paid four lire, 0 soldi to us, Bernardo Saracini and company, which were recorded on page 4 of the book of forced loans and on page 154. L iiii

Benedetto di Meo di Betto has thirty-two lire to pay as rent for the land of the vineyard, that is for the property in Laterino called "the Ghodiuolo," that belongs to San Galgano abbey, as recorded on page 5. L xxxii s 0

He has paid in part as recorded on the same page L 19 s 12

L xviiii s xii

He has paid eight lire, 19 soldi, 4 denari in cash to me, Don Giovanni, on December 13th, 1453, for the year ending on All Hallows 1453. L viii s xviiii d 4

---

1. This is written in the margin.

He owes us twenty-two soldi for early grapes he sold. L 1 s ii

(Page 7) + 1453. On the 12th of January, Meio di Betto called Massarizia paid four lire, 0 soldi to us, Mariano Borghexi and Antonio Pini and associates, recorded on page 3 of the book, on page 165 of forced loans. L 4

On the 28th of February meio di Betto paid four lire, 0 soldi to us, Mariano Borghexi and associates, registered on page 1 of the book of forced loans, with the announcement of February 25th. L 4

On the xxviii of February, Meio paid his forced loan, announced on iiii February, to us, Mariano Borghexi and associates; it is entered on page 153 of the book regarding this forced loan. L 6 s 4

On the xii of April Meio paid his forced loan, announced on March 30th, to us, Mariano Borghesi and associates. The entry is on page 3. L iiii

(Page 7v) 1453. On the first day of March, I, Bartolomeo Ghuidocco, treasury official, received as the "twenty-fourth" tax from Betto 7 lire, 0 soldi, 8 denari, as appears in my entry on page 1, under two accounts; for the oxen tax and for the deadwood tax. L 7 s 0 d 8

(Page 8) + 1454. I, Simone di Francio di Martino, on this day, November 18th, 1454, have received from Betto di Meio di Betto, called "the Massarizia," twenty-eight lire, 0 soldi, as the remainder of a payment for an ox he bought several months ago from Salvestro, my sharecropper at Fonghaia, which was evaluated at fifty-five lire, including twenty-eight lire, twelve soldi, which Bindino di Meo admitted he received from Marcho di Berna, and the same Bindino admits he received them. That is, he owes me another 24 lire, 14 soldi, plus 3 lire, 6 soldi, which are those of Marcho, a total of 21 lire, 0 soldi owed Silvestro from the original 55 lire. The ox, Betto said, he bought for Iachomo del Besso.

(Page 8v) + 1454. On the 28th day of December we, Antonio di Ser Bartolomeio, cloth merchant, have received from Benedetto di Meio, of Montelabuccio, 40 lire, 0 soldi, a part of the 65 lire he owes to the association for animals that we own with Antonio di Francio, involving a couple of heifers, as shown in the booklet of our company on page 60.

And on March 4th we, the same Antonio, have received from the same Benedetto 25 lire, 0 soldi, the remainder owed on the heifers, recorded in the book of our company on page 60.

(*Page 9*) Cristofano di Fortunato, woolworker, is owed on January 4th thirty lire, five soldi, which money is for 1 bed he had delivered to Anto., Paulo di Vitello and company, the cloth peddlers; and so he has become my debtor in his memoir, on page 338. And for these monies I am obliged to pay top quality lime for the whole next month of May, worth 30 lire, 5 soldi, at ten soldi per load delivered to his house in Siena. And he also owes twelve lire and 3 soldi cash on January 4th for 13 1/2 braccia[2] of Romagna-style cloth I procured for him from Lady di Giovanni di Maestro Aghustino.   L xii s iii
And he must have lime of the agreed-upon quality.

(*Page 9v*) + 1454. I, Cristofano di Ser Chele, butcher, received from Benedetto eight lire from Benedetto del Massarizia on February 5th, for 60 pounds of calfs, which Giovanni the tailor[3] had from me until January 25th for Lorenzo, and the balance he owes [   ][4] of Lorenzo the smith [   ] of Petrino the laborer paid on March 9th.

(*Page 10*) 1454. Serafino di Meo, master woodcutter, must have twenty-two lire for an inlaid chest three and a half braccia long, and for a bedstead four and a half by three and a half braccia wide, completely in agreement for these two jobs; and in place of this money I must obtain lime for what is sold, and then on February 15th we will measure the lime, at ten soldi per load as agreed, and he must transport it to me throughout next May; and thus it says in the contract with Serafino, on page 118. And if he should not deliver it by then I am not obliged to accept it.

(*Page 10v*) A memoir of how on xxiiii January 1455 we settled com-

---

2. In the original, the text reads 1/1, by mistake.
3. This is the likeliest reading.
4. The writing in this section has faded to illegibility.

pletely with Benedetto di Meo di Betto for every and all things we had between us regarding the Laterino rent, including replanted vines and everything he did to fix things; in sum, there remain sixteen and a half lire to pay, and he paid them into my hand in the church of the Magdalene with Don Giovanni present. And thus he is quit of every and all dealings with the monastery, as agreed on the day and year above.   L xvi s 10

(Page 11) I, Simone di Francio di Martino, official of the Mirror, received from Betto del Massarizia nineteen lire, nine soldi, as shown in my entry on page 46.

We, Angiolo Baldi and associates, clothiers, received from Benedetto di Meio di Beto on this day, 22nd November, 3 lire, 16 soldi in cash, which he was supposed to pay a long time ago.   L 3 s 16

(Page 11v) On the 21st of August I gave Piero, mayor of the town of Casciano and sharecropper of Pietro di Fabbiano, five soldi, which money is the tax of saint Mary of August.   5 s

Francesco di Matteo di Salvi must receive twenty-two lire, which money Savino di Matteo d'Antonio di Guido, the official of the Council of 24, gave us on this day as part of his salary of the 24.   L 22

Up to the xi day of March, they have given seven lire, twelve soldi, for the wine and wood received.   L 7 s 12

Received twenty-eight soldi for 3 loads of lime on November 9th, 1458.   L 1 s 8

(Page 12) 1459. On the 12th day of August I gave Luca d'Agnolo, mayor of Casciano, five soldi, six denari, which were for the Palio celebrations on the feast of the Virgin in August, and which we owed through the town of Casciano. Giovanni del Massarizia gave them.   5 s 6 d

(Page 12) 1459. Lorenzo di Domenico del Vecchio must receive thirty-three lire, thirteen soldi, 4 denari by August 19th for 202 pounds of Romagna wool at 3 soldi, 4 denari per pound, which is a total of

L 33 s 13 d 4

Up to now he has given five narrow, light wool cloths.   L 25 s 19

He gave on August 19th seven lire, 13 soldi, 4 denari, the balance for the wool. L 7 s 13 d 4

(Page 13) + Christ 1459. On the 27th of January Benedetto paid me back the 4 "broad" fiorini, to me Mariano di Meio di Nardo, which I had loaned him. And I'm fully paid and settled with him. 4 "broad" fiorini

(Page 13v) + Christ 1460. We, Lodovico Tondi, official of the Council of Twenty-Four, have received on this xxviiii of June sixteen lire from Benedetto del Massarizia for [the tax on][5] the wood, the tax on oxen and poles, that is his share. L 16

(Page 14) + Christ 1462. Galgano di Meio di Betto must pay me five and a half lire on the day of February;[6] they are for his half of the 1/4 of the assessment on the animals which he still has to receive from us, a tax which I paid for him to Bartalomeo Benucci. L 5 s 10

And he must pay on the tenth of February seven lire, seven soldi as half of the 14 lire, 14 soldi owed to Ghano Buonagionta, who had loaned that amount for the taxes on woodland. L 7 s 7

And he must pay on the same day twenty-eight soldi and 4 denari, which I paid as his share to Iachomo del Besso as the balance for the lost oxen. L 1 s 8 d 4

Placed on the other side of the page L 14 s 5 d 4

(Page 14v) + Christ 1462. Galgano has to pay fourteen lire and five soldi, 4 denari, which he had to repay on the previous page.

L 14 s 5 d 4

And on February 15th he must pay nineteen soldi, his share which I paid for him of what we owe the Lecceto friars and the children of Betto the grocer. L 0 s 19

(Page 15) + Christ 1463. We, Nofri Borghesi and associates, pay on this 9th day of May 56 lire, 4 soldi, 6 denari to Bartolomeo Benucci on behalf of Betto di Meo di Betto, the sum he had deposited, as proved in the account book, page 48. L 56 s 4 d 6

---

5. A stain here covers the word, which probably was *gabella*.
6. Written between the lines of text.

Appendix

(*Page 15v*) 1471. My lady Chaterina di Silvio Piccolomini must receive on this 9th day of January nineteen lire and 5 soldi, which are for forty-four staia of wheat Benedetto di Massaricia got to sow in Sticiano, as agreed with my lady Chaterina. L 19 s 5
The aforesaid lady Chaterina has received 15 lire and 15 soldi, counted.
L 15 s 15

(*Page 16*) + 1474. I, Antonio di Tinghoccio the spicer, official of Lucignano, have received four lire, one soldo from Benedetto del Massarizia on behalf of his son Francesco, for the tax on the holding at Montefurelo, in the township of Santo Sano, for the six-month period begun on the calends of January and ending on the calends of July 1474.
L 4 s 1

(*Page 16v*) + 1475. Giovanni di Tognio, resident of Villa a Piano, must receive ten gold ducats, full wide, which are for the ox he sold in June to Benedetto de Massaritia for the aforesaid ten ducats.
And the same Giovanni di Tognio declares himself paid and settled with Benedetto for that ox as of this 18th October. And I, Pasquino di Jachomo di Pasquino the grocer have made this written note, as both parties requested, for they do not know how to write.

(*Page 17*) + 1475. And I, Iachomo Pini, have received 4 lire from Benedetto de Masaritia for lady Giovanna degli Schotti, as he promised our Giovanni Pini. L 4
These are for a hayfield sold at Bascani.

(*Page 17v*) + Christ, on the 26th October 1475. I, Francesco Belliarmati, official of the town, have received today, the day mentioned above, nine lire, eight soldi, owed by Benedetto del Massarizia as tax on his kiln, and they are recorded in the income on page 127.
The same, on xiiii November, 4 lire, 14 soldi, recorded on page 10.

L 9 s 8

We, Benedetto Cieloni, received today, October 28th, from Benedetto del Massariza, thirteen lire, fifteen soldi, counted by the teacher Alisandro, which are for II pigs he got from us, and for which he owes, as recorded in book C, page 265. L 13 s 15

(*Page 18*) + Christ 1475. I Pauolo di Tomasso di Pauolo, goldsmith, received on this 2nd December seventeen lire, 19 soldi, the total I was owed by Benedetto del Massaritia, who lives at Marciano in the Masse of Siena, and this money is for a belt and buckles of gilt silver which he got from me, as shown in my booklet on page 70.　　L 17 s 19
I also received 2 soldi to cover expenses for obtaining payment.

(*Page 18v*) + June 29th, 1476. Betto del Massaritia from Marciano paid three lire as his tax on oxen to Francesco di Fatio Belarmato, official for beasts of burden, recorded on page 13 of the account book. In addition he paid twenty soldi to Francesco Belarmatto as his tax on stones, recorded on page 22.

(*Page 19*) 1476. On the 22nd of August I, lord Domenico Francesconi, receive thirty-five lire in money from Benedetto del Massarizia for the daughter of Tome di Nofrio and lady Agnesa his wife, as appears on page 43 of the book of lord Lorenzo Bonelli. These monies are owed to Giovanni, son of this Tome.

(*Page 19v*) 1476. Benedetto di Cristofano Palmieri, of Prata di Maremma, exchanged with us 1 heifer for an old ox, and he owes us a heifer, and we agreed that we would pay him twenty-one lire in addition for the heifer; and of this money I pay right now two "broad" ducats, and later I had three lire and two soldi, which he received in shoes from Simone di Stefano.　　L 14 s 6
He received on the ninth of October six lire and fourteen soldi in cash, paid into his palm in the presence of Tonio Ciconi and Francesco di Pipio di Nicolo d'Orsino of Marciano. And this Benedetto di Cristofano declares himself paid and settled with before these witnesses.

L 6 s 14

(*Page 20*) + 1476. Benedetto di Meo di Betto must receive on this day, xxviii of December, forty-eight lire, two soldi, which are for cloth he took from us, shown in their records on page 132; and we testify he has finished paying. And I, Nicholo d'Antonio di Ricciardo, swear this as their fellow shopkeeper.

We, Marco Benzi and associates, received on this 28th of January four lire from Benedetto del Massarizia, a downpayment on the xii lire he owes us and he may pay all to me, Piertro di Ser Mariano.　　L 4
and on the x February six lire to our Matteo　　L 6
(Page 20v) + Christ 1476. We, the cloth peddlers Francesco Petrocci and company, swear to Benedetto di Meo del Massarizia from Marciano that we have received forty-five soldi, 8[7] denari in cash as payment in full of all debts at our shop up to this day, viii February; and we returned to the same Benedetto one tablecloth, 8 braccia long, quite threadbare, 5 towels sown together, 6 napkins sown together, 1 used women's cotton cloth. And in this way he settled his account in our yellow book, on page 44.　　L 2 s 5

(Page 21) I, Giovanni di Messer Austino, received on this day, February 28th, from Benedetto del Massarizia, 4 lire, 4 soldi, as the remainder of 36 lire which Cirevagio di Chaterino and Pietro di Benedetto owed us for clothes they got from us.

(Page 21v) + 1476. I, Benedetto di Meo di Betto del Massarizia, have given and paid today, March first, have given and paid cash to Francesco di Borsello of Coscona three lire, one soldo as payment in full of all our outstanding debts with him up to this day.　　L 3 s 1
And I, Giovanni d'Ugulino, made this entry as they pleaded, because they do not know how to write.

(Page 22) 22 + Christ, mcccclxxvi. We, Marco Benzi and company, received today, March vi, forty soldi from Benedetto del Massarizia, the balance from twelve lire he owed us, and they are recorded on his account in my big yellow book,[8] "D," on page 34 under Master Bertoccio Tholomei.　　L 2

(Page 22v) + Christ 1479. Giovanni Lapini and Paolo, his son and my son-in-law, who currently live on the edge of Uvile in their own house,

---

7. 8 appears over a crossed out 4.
8. This is the likeliest reading of the abbreviation here.

are owed sixty-two lire on November xxvi, which are for a hooded gown of French-style cloth, like new, one bed, one bedstead like new, assessed by Guido di Simone, jacket-maker, and Fruosino di Finuccio, as recorded by the contract drawn up by Bernardino Placiti, which is, by common agreement, a portion of the dowry of my daughter Bernardina, as I promised.   L 62

(Page 23) + Christ 1479. We, Mateo di Ser Arduino and associates, cloth peddlers, received today, December 15th, six lire, sixteen soldi, or L 6 s 16, from Benedetto, the balance of his debt before today.

L 6 s 16

(Page 23v) + 1499. I, Girolamo di Lagniaia, received on this 26th of December from Pietro del Massarizia ten gold ducats, which he had gotten from Iacomo de Ragnitegli as his part of the dowry of his daughter Lisabetta.

(Page 24) + Christ, on the xxvi day of March, 1499. Pietro di Benedetto del Massarizia paid us, Birighucci the bankers, fifty-three lire as toll on viii some of wine, recorded in the book of entries, page 135.

And he sent 16 staia of wine today   4 some of wine.

And he sent on March 28th he sent   1 some of wine.

And he sent on April 2nd   3 some of wine.

(Page 24v) + Christ, on the 4th day of April 1500. Pietro di Benedetto del Massarizia paid four lire, 0 soldi to us Birighucci the banker, as toll on xxiiii of wine, recorded on page 135 of the entries book.

He sent today 4 staia of wine.

He sent on April 9th 4 staia of wine.

And he sent on the xviii of the same month 2 staia of wine

2 staia of wine.

And he sent on the 4th of June eight staia of wine   8 staia of wine.

He stored on June 20th 4 staia of wine.

(Page 25) + Christ 1500. Pietro di Benedetto del Massarizia paid us, Biringhucci, nine lire, sixteen soldi, as toll on xxviii of wine, in the entries 3.

On February 16th he sent 3 some of wine.

On the 17th he sent 3 some of wine.

On the same day he sent two some of wine.

On March 23rd he sent 4 staia	1 soma of wine.
On April v he sent 1 soma of wine	4 staia of wine.
On April 23rd he sent 1 soma of wine	4 staia of wine.
And on May 9th he sent 1 soma of wine	4 staia of wine.
On June 7th he sent one soma of wine	4 staia of wine.
On the same day he sent two some of wine	8 staia of wine.
On the 7th he sent one soma, 1 staio	v staia of wine.
And on July 31st he sent	4 staia of wine.

(*Page 25*) + Christ, on the xxviii of February 1501. Today Pietro di Benedetto Massarizia paid us, Nicolo Piccolomini and company, ten lire, six soldi, 8 denari as toll on xxxi some of wine.   L 10 s 6 8.
Girolamo Bargagli, chamberlain.

On the last day of April he sent one soma of wine,

and on May 7th he sent 4 staia of wine	1 soma of wine,

And on May 13th he sent 1 soma of wine,

And on May 17th he sent 4 some of wine.

On the 18th of the same month, he sent two some of wine	
	2 some of wine.
On the same day he sent two some of wine	2 some of wine,
And on the same day he sent	2 some of wine.

(*Page 26*) + I, Master Emanuello, guardian of the convent and friars of S. Francesco in Siena. In my own name and in the name of the convent and friars, I declare myself debtor and payer on behalf of the convent, to Pietro di Benedetto di Massarizia who lives in Marciano in the Masse of Siena, of sixty-five lire, that is 65 lire in Sienese money. They are for the ten some of scarlet wine which we buy from him for the friar's convent; and I promise to pay this money on the day seven[9] of next

---

9. Written over a crossed out 8.

June. And, as a pledge of this, I wrote this contract with my own hand on May 18th, 1502; he corrected the "seven" since I promised that amount in "broad" ducats, that is L 14
He got forty-three lire in several installments, and today, October 7th L 43
Meo, son of this Pietro, received as the final installment eight lire, and is fully satisfied by the convent of S. Francesco through me, Master Luca the guardian. L 8

(*Page 26v*) 1502. Pietro Massarizia brought five some of bread.
5 some.

(*Page 27v*) On the xvii May, 1503. Pietro di Benedetto pays four lire, as toll on xii some of wine; in cash to me, Giovanni. L 4

(*Page 89*) 1453. On September 24th Meio di Betto paid four lire as forced loan to us, Riciardo Saracini, as revealed in the book of forced loans on page 183. L 4

On July 20th Benedetto di Meio di Betto paid nine lire, eight soldi to us, Galghano Bichi, recorded on page 209 of the book, and as income on page 2. L 9 s 8

On August xvii Benedetto di Meio di Betto paid us, Galghano Bichi, 9 lire, eight soldi as forced loan on the second loan for Pitigliano, and they are recorded in the book of loans, page 165.

(*Page 89v*) On January 31st Meio di Betto del Massarizia paid Nicolo Angelo Pacini the chamberlain twenty lire in many installments, as recorded in the book of forest resources, page 56; they were a tax on the kiln. L 20

(*Page 93v*) 1502. Pietro Massarizia brought nine some of bread. Girolamo.

Notes

All the documents used in this study are in the state archive of Siena. Hence I deemed it unnecessary to cite their exact location each time. *Notarile* indicates that the document came from the *Notarile ante-cosimiano* collection; *Patrimonio resti* means the *Patrimonio dei resti ecclesiastici* created by the suppression of religious companies and confraternities in 1785; the *Balia* collection contains documents generated by the civic office of the same name (for the history of this magistracy, see the introduction by G. Prunai and S. De' Colli in *Archivio di Balia: Inventario* [Rome, 1957], ix–lxxxi); and the series called *Bocche* is that part of the *Balia* documentation where various populations censuses taken between 1523 and 1598 are kept. The memoirs of the grocer Giovanni di Niccolò di Ranieri are in the collection called *Ospedale di Santa Maria della Scala*, number 1176. Subtitles of published works in Italian are omitted.

Introduction by Muir

1. D. Herlihy and C. Klapisch-Zuber, *The Tuscans and Their Families: A Study of the Florentine Catasto of 1427* (New Haven, 1985); C. Klapisch-Zuber, *Women, Family, and Ritual in Renaissance Italy*, trans. L. G. Cochrane (Chicago, 1985); and A. Molho, *Marriage Alliance in Late Medieval Florence* (Cambridge, Mass., 1994).

2. J. C. Scott, *Weapons of the Weak: Everyday Forms of Peasant Resistance* (New Haven, 1985) and *Domination and the Arts of Resistance: Hidden Transcripts* (New Haven, 1990).

Introduction by Balestracci

1. G. Cherubini, "Una famiglia di piccoli proprietari contadini del territorio di Castrocare (1383–1384)," in his *Signori, contadini, borghesi* (Florence, 1974), 467.

2. A. Momigliano, "Linee per una valutazione della storiografia del quindicennio, 1961–1976," *Rivista storica italiana* 89 (1977): 596.

3. C. Ginzburg, *The Cheese and the Worms: The Cosmos of a Sixteenth-Century Miller*, trans. J. and A. Tedeschi (Baltimore, 1980), xv.

4. E. Le Roy Ladurie, *Montaillou: The Promised Land of Error*, trans. B. Bray (New York, 1979), vii.

5. With the exception of peasants' declarations to the fifteenth-century Florentine *Catasto* or Sienese *Lira*, surviving testimonies from country people are few.

6. Medieval Italian account books and diaries that have been edited or used by historians are limited to the following: *Ricordi di una famiglia senese del secolo decimoterzo*, a faulty edition of a diary from the thirteenth century, and the *Ricordi di Cristofano Guidini*, an incomplete nineteenth-century edition of the diary of this Sienese notary and disciple of St. Catherine, recently studied by Cherubini ("Dal libro di conti di un notaio senese del Trecento" in his *Signori, contadini, borghesi*). The diary of a Cortonese merchant, Niccoluccio di Cecco della Boccia, who lived in Siena in the second half of the Trecento, was the basis for Sandra Tortoli's "Il podere e i mezzadri di Niccoluccio di Cecco della Boccia, mercante cortonese a Siena" (*Ricerche storiche* 10 [1980]: 239—84); her notes mention the existence of other such books by the woolworkers Minuccio di Naldo, Fabiano Palmieri (240), and Cristoforo Pestelli; by the grocer Giovanni di Niccolò Ranieri; by the nephew of Niccoluccio della Boccia, Antonio di Carlo; and by the dyer Landoccio di Cecco d'Orso (241n). See Tortoli's work for the archival references. The latter source was used in the university thesis of Piero Guarducci, who then re-used this same book of accounts for his study, "Semilavoratori ferrosi nella Toscana del sec. XIV," *Ricerche storiche* 10 (1980): 613—18. Another private book of accounts, by the Sienese merchant Dino de' Marzi who flourished around 1400 (preserved in the Archivio di Siena, *Patrimonio resti* 2.344), served as the documentary base for the thesis of Zoraide Gobbini Arcese ("Il memoriale di Dino de' Marzi, mercante senese, dal 1395 al 1427," thesis, Faculty of Letters and Philosophy, University of Siena, 1980—81). There is a book of expenses by a woman named Monna Bartolomea, also kept in the Sienese archive and dating to the early fifteenth century (*Notarile*, 271). Preserved in several manuscripts in the Biblioteca Comunale degli Intronati of the same city are the diary of Giovanni Battista di ser Simone da Ricodoli, kept by various members of the family from 1286 to 1513 (A.VII.32), and the administrative account book kept by Domenico di Cecco for Riccardo and Giovanni Saracini from 1462 and 1466 (A.VI.39).

7. C. De la Roncière's comments on Lippo di Fede del Sega, a Florentine moneychanger of the 1300s, apply (*Un changeur florentin du Trecento: Lippo di Fede del Sega* [Paris, 1973], 7): in this case he was able to investigate the life of a bourgeois of small fortune, to discover who he was and how he lived while working at the same trade as the Scali or Peruzzi without reaching their level. In the case of Benedetto, we see a category of country people living beyond brutish, desperate poverty.

8. This fusion of writing and city is largely real. Yet, as A. Bartoli Langeli warned several years ago, it should not "discourage," nor should it be taken as axiomatic (see his introduction in *Alfabetismo e cultura scritta nella storia della società italiana* [Perugia, 1978], 30). The very concept of writing as a "frontier element" between city and country has by now several acknowledged exceptions (see S. Gasparri, *Un curriculo di storia non urbana* [Florence, 1982], 22).

9. Le Roy Ladurie, *Montaillou*, 6. See also Cherubini, "Vita trecentesca nelle novelle di Giovanni Sercambi," in his *Signori, contadini, borghesi*, 40.

10. These equivalencies were calculated using the *Tavole di ragguaglio per la riduzione dei pesi e delle misure che si usano nella città di Siena al peso e misura vegliante in Firenze* (Siena, 1783).

11. A. K. Isaacs, "Popolo e Monti nella Siena del primo Cinquecento," *Rivista storica italiana* 82 (1970): 35–36.

12. W. M. Bowsky, *The Finance of the Commune of Siena, 1287–1355* (Oxford, 1970), 114–65.

13. Ibid., 166–88.

14. Ibid., 2.

1. A Region with Pen in Hand

1. On Tuscan mercantile activity in Europe, see A. Sapori, "La cultura del mercante italiano," vol. 2, esp. 67–68, and "La mercatura medievale," vol. 1, esp. 33–34, and his articles "La compagnia dei Frescobaldi in Inghilterra," vol. 1, 859–926, and "Le compagnie italiane in Inghilterra," vol. 2, 1039–70, all in his *Studi di storia economica* (Florence 1961). See also Y. Renouard, *Gli uomini d'affari italiani nel Medioevo* (Milan, 1973), 165–231. All these contain useful bibliographies. On merchant culture, D. De Robertis, "L'esperienza poetica del Quattrocento," in *Storia della letteratura italiana*, vol. 3 (Milan, 1966), 377, states "the long, loving, obscure daily exercise of personal writings, memoirs, commercial and business documents [typified the Quattrocento]. Of course, this was no rare and exceptional effort, but a huge production, mostly still unpublished, that no one has yet dared to measure. Florence was the epicenter of the phenomenon." On the political triumphs of the urban classes, see Y. Renouard, *Le città italiane dal X al XIV secolo* (Milan, 1975), vol. 1, 212–63 on Pisa and vol. 2, 96–119 on Florence. On Florence, see the classics, G. Salvemini, *Magnati e Popolani in Firenze dal 1280 al 1295* (Milan, 1966), N. Ottokar, *Il Comune di Firenze alla fine del Dugento* (Torino, 1966); R. Davidsohn, *L'egemonia guelfa e la vittoria del popolo*, vol. 2 of *Storia de Firenze* (Florence, 1972), esp. 537–80. On Siena, see W. M. Bowsky's *A Medieval Italian Commune: Siena under the Nine, 1287–1355* (Berkeley, 1981).

2. C. Bec, *Les marchands écrivains: Affaires et humanisme à Florence, 1375–1434* (Paris, 1967), 439.

3. Ibid., p. 50.

4. Neri di Bicci, *Le ricordanze (10 marzo 1453–24 aprile 1475),* ed. B. Santi (Pisa, 1976), 1. G. Morelli, *Ricordi*, ed. A. Schiaffini (Florence, 1969), 81, and Cristofano di Gano di Guidino (395) give personal and family glory as their motivations for writing.

5. F. Cardini, "Alfabetismo e cultura scritta nell'età comunale: Alcuni problemi," in *Alfabetismo e cultura scritta nella storia della società italiana* (Perugia, 1978), 184.

6. M. Berengo, *Nobili e mercanti nella Lucca del Cinquecento* (Torino, 1965), 74.

7. As A. Bartoli Langeli put it, "The history of culture is more marked by exclusions, negations, closures than by developments and broadenings. Yet this need not imply that all writing expresses dominant culture" ("Premesse," *Quaderni storici* 13 [1978]: 450). See also his "Intervento di apertura," in *Alfabetismo e cultura scritta*, 30–31, and A. Petrucci, "Per la storia dell'alfabetismo e della cultura scritta: Metodi-materiali-quesiti," in *Alfabetismo e cultura scritta*, 33–47.

8. See P. Lucchi, "La Santacroce, il Salterio e il Babuino: Libri per imparare a leggere nel primo secolo della stampa," *Quaderni storici* 13 (1978): 605. C. De la Roncière, *Florence*, vol. 3 (Aix-en-Provence, 1976), 1085–86, mentions some interesting examples of people from Florence's hinterland in the fourteenth century who could barely write but did not renounce the world of writing, and others who were fully literate (see also Petrucci, "Per la storia," 36). On readers who did not write, see D. Marchesini, "Sposi e scolari," *Quaderni Storici* 18 (1983): 604. In general on the composite world of literacy and semiliteracy among the lower classes, see C. M. Cipolla's pioneering work, *Literacy and Development in the West* (Harmondsworth, Eng., 1969), fundamental to medieval studies. See also P. Burke, *Popular Culture in Early Modern Europe* (Aldershot, Eng., 1994), esp. 250–52; the Perugia seminar of 1977 on literacy (*Alfabetismo e cultura scritta*); Petrucci's "Per la storia," esp. 453–54, 490; his "Nota sulla scrittura di Angela Mellini," *Quaderni storici* 14 (1979): 640, and his "Scrittura e alfabetismo ed educazione grafica nella Roma del primo Cinquecento," *Scrittura e civiltà* 2 (1978): 193–94; and also A. Bartoli Langeli's "Culture grafiche e competenze testuali nel Quattro-Cinquecento italiano" in *Retorica e classi sociali* (Padua, 1983), 84.

9. See O. Cavallo, "Dal segno incompiuto al segno negato," in *Alfabetismo e cultura scritta*, 120.

10. Ibid., 140.

11. Bartoli Langeli, "Culture grafiche," 91.

12. See F. H. Bauml, "Varieties and Consequences of Medieval Literacy and Illiteracy," *Speculum* 55 (1980): 237–65. Both C. M. Cipolla (*Before the Industrial Revolution: European Society and Economy, 1000–1700* [New York, 1980], 146–49, 178), who believes that the elementary culture of the Middle Ages was urban and reached the countryside only in the eighteenth century, and then only in Protestant areas, while Catholic peasants remained illiterate, and R. S. Lopez (*La nascita dell'Europa: Secoli V–XIV* [Torino, 1966], 309), who says that in Italy's rural areas the custom of writing had begun to take root as early as the 1200s, are right. By around 1250, English peasants of diverse levels were making growing use of writing and written documents. Thus M. T. Clanchy, *From Memory to Written Record: England 1066–1307* (Cambridge, Mass., 1979), 34–38, could suppose that the fourteenth-century English countryside had a literacy rate at least equal to Lombardy's.

13. M. S. Mazzi and S. Raveggi, *Gli uomini e le cose nelle campagne fiorentine del Quattrocento* (Florence, 1983), 210–11, 240, 278–80, 303.

14. Cited by R. Hirsch, "Stampa e lettura fra il 1450 e il 1550," in *Libri, editori e pubblico nell'Europa moderna: Guida storica e critica*, ed. A. Petrucci (Bari, 1977), 47–50.

15. Cipolla, *Literacy*, 46, maintains that "we cannot overlook the fact that during the thirteenth and fourteenth centuries numerous minor cities and rural centers in Italy established schools and hired lay teachers." A. K. Isaacs, "Le campagne senesi fra Quattro e Cinquecento," in *Contadini e proprietari nella Toscana moderna*, vol. 1 (Florence, 1979), 381, mentions the mountain schools of Siena's hinterland in the fifteenth and sixteenth centuries. Burke, *Popular Culture*, 29–36, discusses in general the differences between various situations in the countryside.

16. It is worth mentioning tiny Bucine's statutes of 1411, which refer to grammar teachers (see C. Mazzi, "Cartiere, tipografie e maestri di grammatica in Valdelsa," in *Carta e cartiere a Colle* [Florence, 1982], 129). For the statutes of Castelfranco di Sopra, from 1394, see *Statuti dei comuni di Castelfranco di Sopra (1394) Castighone degli Ubertini (1397)*, ed. G. Caneani Marti (Florence, 1963), 58. In 1360 Montopoli had a "magister" who lived there "ad docendum pueros" (*Statuto del comune di Montopoli [1360]*, ed. B. Casini [Florence, 1968], 109–10, 337). Throughout the sixteenth century there seem to have always been teachers in the main villages of Mount Amiata; Casteldelpiano paid a teacher in 1571 "to teach the children of everyone properly" (*Statuti di Castel del Piano sul Monte Amiata [1571]*, ed. I. Imberciadori [Florence, 1980], 351). And in 1592 Campagnatilo spent 3.5 percent of its budget on education, Abbadia San Salvatore 4 percent, Montepescali 4.5 percent, and Torrita 6 percent (I. Imberciadori, *Per la storia della società: Amiata e Maremma* [Parma, 1971], 223–24).

17. E. Conti, *I catasti agrari della Repubblica fiorentina e il catasto particellare toscano (secoli XIV–XIX)* (Rome, 1966), 85, with note on the statutes of Gangalandi (Lastra a Signa); *Statuti dei comuni di Castelfranco di Sopra*, 58.

18. *Statuto del comune di Santa Maria al Monte (1391)*, ed. B. Casini (Florence, 1961), 199.

19. *Statuti dei comuni di Castelfranco di Sopra*, 58.

20. See P. Ariès, *Padri e figli nell'Europa medievale e moderna* (Bari, 1968), 157.

21. See G. Fioravanti, *Università e città*, (Florence, 1981), 33, 35, 50–51, 98, on a Sienese teacher who went to teach in rural schools. G. Petti Balbi, *L'insegnamento nella Liguria medievale* (Genoa, 1979) offers comparative data on teaching in another region's hamlets.

22. Piovano Arlotto, *Novelle*, no. 35, in *Novelle del Quattrocento*, ed. G. Ferrero and M. Doglio (Turin, 1975), 759.

23. Clanchy, *From Memory*, 217, discusses literacy acquired from listening instead of reading. See also N. Zemon Davis, *Society and Culture in Early Modern France* (Stanford, 1975), 195–96.

24. C. Ginzburg, *The Cheese and the Worms: The Cosmos of a Sixteenth-Century Miller*, trans. J. and A. Tedeschi (Baltimore, 1980), 97.

25. Cipolla, *Literacy*, 42, notes that "written documents replace oral tradition in a growing number of agrarian contracts, as society and economy became more dynamic, commercialized, and even rural areas were affected by the trend." See also De la Roncière, *Florence*, vol. 3, 1084–86.

26. Oderigo di Credi, *Ricordanze di Oderigo di Andrea di Credi, orafo, cittadino fiorentino*, ed. F. Polidori, in *Archivio storico italiano* 4 (1843): 75, 79, 82.

27. *Memorie di Giovanni di Niccolo di Ranieri Speziale*, August 29, 1431, chap. 169 (see note 6 to the introduction, above).

28. See F. Cardini, "Alfabetismo," 185; M. Vovelle, "Storia e lunga durata," in *La nuova storia*, ed. J. Le Goff (Milan, 1980), 60; and Ginzburg's introduction to the Italian edition of P. Burke, *Cultura popolare* (Milan, 1980), xiv.

29. G. Duby, *L'arte e la società medievale* (Bari, 1977), 233. Writing about sixteenth-century Rome, A. Petrucci ("Scrittura e alfabetismo ed educazione grafica nella Roma del primo

Cinquecento" *Scrittura e civiltà* 2 [1978], 184) argues that "the use of writing was evidently seen as socially relevant even at the lowest socioeconomic levels. This is demonstrated not only by the presumed prestige public writers held, but also by the case of the cheesemaker Braccio who tried to avoid the need to delegate writing to others and to prove his clumsy literacy."

30. On the satire against peasants, see the old but still partially valid D. Merlini, *Satira contro il villano* (Turin, 1894), and more recently, E. Sereni, "Agricoltura e mondo rurale," in *Storia d'Italia*, vol. 1 (Turin, 1972), 193–96; G. Giorgetti, *Contadini e proprietari nell'Italia moderna*, (Turin, 1974), 42; G. Cherubini, "La Signoria dei Cerretani dul castello maremmano di Stertignano," in his *Signori, contadini, borghesi*, 192–99 and his "Il mondo contadino," in *Medioevo rurale*, ed. V. Criagelli and E. Rossetti (Bologna, 1980), 425–28. Specifically on *baccalare* as "presumptuous" or "know-it-all," see G. Piccinni, *"Seminare, fruttare, raccogliere"* (Milan, 1982), 220.

31. G. Sermini, *Novelle*, no. 25, ed. G. Vettori, 433.

32. Paolo di Pace, *Libro di buoni costumi*, ed. A. Schiaffini (Florence, 1945), 144.

33. Bauml, "Medieval Literacy," 246.

34. Conti, *I catasti*, 85.

35. As F. Cardini, "Sui catasti fiorentini e altro," *Notizie: Alfabetismo e culture scritta. Seminario permanente* (March 1980), 12, also puts it, "the community of writers . . . is in fact a 'community of speakers,' of 'orators,' of 'gesticulators.'"

36. See Petrucci, "Scrittura e alfabetismo," 182–83, and "Per la storia," 453, on such cases.

37. Ibid., 183.

38. A 16v.

39. A 21v.

40. B 26–26v.

41. See Cavallo, "Dal segno incompiuto," 134.

42. Petrucci, "Scrittura e alfabetismo," 179.

2. "Luscious Valleys" and "Magnificent Villas"

1. E. Repetti, in *Dizionario geografico fisico storico della Toscana*, vol. 3 (Rome, 1838), 180, writes "Masse . . . has been applied to the various places of Tuscany in two senses; either in the sense which the stony nature of the soil, with its great rocks or 'masse' supplied, or in the geographic sense of a cluster of houses owned by the same person; in the latter sense 'masse' was applied also to districts with scattered houses close to, close upon, or adjacent to cities." Siena's Masse correspond to Lucca's *Sei miglia*, Arezzo's *Cortine*, Brescia's *Chiusure*, or Vicenza's *Colture*; see M. Berengo, "Le città d'antico regime," in *Dalla città preindustriale alla città del capitalismo*, ed. A. Caracciolo (Bologna, 1975), 49.

2. See R. Stopani, *Il rinnovamento dell'edilizia rurale* (Florence, 1982), 6, and G. F. Di Pietro, "Per la storia dell'architettura della dimora rurale," *Archeologia medievale* 7 (1980): 347–48.

3. On rural houses, see Stopani, *Rinnovamento*, 15; G. Salvagnini, *Resedi rurali in Toscana* (Florence, 1980), 41; R. Biasutti, *La casa rurale nella Toscana* (Bologna, 1938), esp. 98–104.

4. G. Piccinni and R. Francovich, "Aspetti del popolamento e del paesaggio nelle campagne senesi bassomedievali," in *I castelli del senese*, vol. 2 (Milan, 1976), 266; G. Cherubini, "Il paesaggio agrario" in *Città e regione* (January 1976), 39.

5. See R. Stopani, *Medievali "case da signore"* (Florence, 1978), 26 and 17; G. Cherubini, "Risorse, paesaggio ed utilizzazione agricola del territorio della Toscana sud-occidentale," in *Civiltà ed economia agricola* (Pistoia, 1981), 100 and his "Le campagne italiane dall'XI al XV secolo," in *Storia d'Italia*, vol. 4 (Turin, 1981), 427; also G. Pinto, "Le strutture ambientali e le basi dell'economia rurale," in his *La Toscana nel tardo Medioevo* (Florence, 1982), 37; and C. Klapisch-Zuber, "Mezzadria e insediamenti rurali alla fine del medio evo," in *Civiltà ed economia agricola*, 156.

6. Eneas Silvius Piccolomini, *Memoirs of a Renaissance Pope*, ed. L. Gabel, trans. F. Gragg (New York, 1959), 4, 154–55.

7. To evaluate the stereotypical element in this description, compare Bonvesin de la Riva, *Le meragivlie di Milano* (Milan, 1974), 45–47 on Milan, and Giovanni Villani, *Cronica*, vol. 11 (Turin, 1979), 94, 212–13, or Leonardo Bruni, *Panegirico* (Florence, 1974), 25 on Florence.

8. *Gabella contratti*, 307, August 2, 1493, 15v.

9. See P. Cammarosano and V. Passeri, "Repertorio," in *I castelli del senese*, vol. 2, 339, 389–90; Piccinni and Francovich, "Aspetti del popolamento," 264; Repetti, *Dizionario storico*, vol. 1, 294; vol. 2, 665–66.

10. G. Giorgetti, *Le crete senesi nell'età moderna* (Turin, 1974), 61–62.

11. Cherubini, "Il paesaggio," 38.

12. See G. Cherubini, "Proprietari, contadini e campagne senesi all'inizio del Trecento," in his *Signori, contadini, borghesi* (Florence, 1974), 263–74, 278–80, 288; Pinto, "Le strutture ambientali," 37. See M. Berengo, *Nobili e mercanti nella Lucca del Cinquecento* (Torino, 1965), 294, 302–6, on the many similarities between the Masse and Lucca's *Sei miglia*.

13. See Pinto, "Le strutture ambientali," 35, 38–39.

14. I. Imberciadori, *Mezzadria classica toscana* (Florence, 1951) analyzes the normative sharecropping relations.

15. G. Giorgetti, *Contadini e proprietari nell'Italia moderna* (Turin, 1974).

16. See R. Stopani, *Villaggi rurali nel Chianti* (Florence, 1981), 21–23, on the Chianti in this same period, where peasants also inhabited villages.

17. Ibid., 12–14.

18. See O. Redon, "I comuni," in *Uomini e comunità del contado senese nel Duecento* (Siena, 1982), 177.

19. See the map in ibid.

20. See Repetti, *Dizionario storico*, vol. 3, 180–81.

21. W. M. Bowsky, *The Finance of the Commune of Siena, 1287–1355* (Oxford, 1970), 170.

22. A. K. Isaacs, "Le campagne senesi fra Quattro e Cinquecento," in *Contadini e proprietari nella Toscana moderna*, vol. 1 (Florence, 1979), 393–94.

23. Repetti, *Dizionario storico,* vol. 5, 380.

24. Bowsky, *Finance,* 246.

25. For the variety of systems peasants employed to obtain land, see P. Jones, "From Manor," in *Florentine Studies,* ed. N. Rubinstein (London, 1968), 234–36; E. Conti, *La formazione della struttura agraria,* vol. 1 (Rome, 1966), 3, 12; Giorgetti, *Contadini e proprietari,* 62; Imberciadori, *Mezzadria classica toscana,* 68; and L. A. Kotel'nikova, "Condizione economica," in *Domanda e consumi, livelli e strutture,* ed. V. Barbagli Bagnoli (Florence, 1978), 96. See Giorgetti, *Le crete,* 105–6, on the loss of common identity by peasant communities, and on the weakening of the parish, the main "coagulator" of community, in a later period.

26. Repetti, *Dizionario storico,* vol. 5, 380–81, calculates that in 1318 there were 1,572 persons responsible for paying the lira tax, plus two friaries and one nunnery, in the Terzo di Città segment of the Masse; 1,243 taxpayers and four male and five female monasteries in the Terzo di San Martino segment of the Masse; and 1,310 taxpayers with four male and two female monasteries in the Terzo di Camollia segment.

27. See Piccinni and Francovich, "Aspetti del popolamento," 266.

28. Ibid., 269 in the notes. See also Pinto, "Le strutture ambientali," 69 and G. Piccinni, "I 'villani incittadinati' nell Siena del XIV secolo," *Bullettino senese di storia patria* 82–83 (1975–76): 195.

29. See S. Tortoli, "Il podere e i mezzadri di Niccoluccio di Cecco della Boccia, mercante cortonese a Siena," *Ricerche storiche* 10 (1980): 279. Sharecroppers suffered most from the insecure conditions, for the cost of reconstruction after the incursions fell almost wholly upon them (see G. De' Rossi, "Sviluppo economico e agricoltura," in *Un'altra Firenze* [Florence, 1971], 10).

30. Piccinni and Francovich, "Aspetti del popolamento," 269 in the notes.

31. M. Ginatempo, "Crisi di un territorio," thesis, University of Siena, Faculty of Letters and Philosophy, 1982–83.

32. See Pinto, "Le strutture ambientali," 79–80.

33. Cherubini, "Risorse," 109; Piccinni, "I 'villani incittadinati,'" 196; Piccinni and Francovich, "Aspetti del popolamento," 266.

34. Pinto, "Le strutture ambientali," 69.

35. Ginatempo, "Crisi di un Territorio."

36. O. Malavolti, *Dell'historia di Siena* (Venice, 1599; rpt. Bologna, 1968), pt. 3, bk. 2, 42–42v.

37. Ibid., 74.

38. *Lira,* 200 (1481); 204 (1483).

3. A Village Bourgeoisie

1. M. S. Mazzi and S. Raveggi, "Masserizie contadine nella prima metà del Quattrocento," in *Civiltà ed economia agricola* (Pistoia, 1981), 195, write that "the peasant world has yet another credit still pending from historians, so careful to investigate the hundreds of incar-

nations of urban people but who have also long been willing to accept a schematic and static portrait of the country."

2. M. S. Mazzi and S. Raveggi, *Gli uomini e le cose nelle campagne fiorentine del Quattrocento* (Florence, 1983), 19, note "inequality and difference in the huge, heterogeneous group of rural workers, and not only between social classes but also within the same class."

3. See P. Toubert, *Les structures du Latium médiéval: Le Latium méridional et la Sabine du IX à la fin du XIIe siècle*, vol. 1 (Rome, 1973), 700.

4. D. Herlihy and C. Klapisch-Zuber, *The Tuscans and Their Families: A Study of the Florentine Catasto of 1427* (New Haven, 1985), 350–51.

5. See C. Klapisch-Zuber, "Mezzadria e insediamenti rurali all fine del medio evo," in *Civiltà ed economia agricola*, 166. Herlihy and Klapisch-Zuber, *Tuscans*, 351, claim family names were more common in richer, less strictly agricultural districts.

6. *Notarile*, 706, March 12, 1484, fasc. 3.

7. B 10, 12; *Notarile*, 656, October 30, 1479, number 34.

8. See J. Delumeau, *La Peur en Occident* (Paris, 1978), 165. Occasional purchases of fish (B 38v) and young ox or veal (A 9v), do not show us all of the foods, beyond those produced by their fields, that reached their table.

9. In a community from the Tuscan part of the Apennine mountains, there were similar gradations of peasant wealth: see G. Cherubini, *Una comunità dell'Appennino* (Florence, 1972), 116.

10. Note, e.g., the case studied by L. De Angelis, "Intorno all 'attività di Deo di Guono," *Archeologia medievale* 3 (1976): 429–46, of a smith from the Casentino area who preponderantly repaired old farming equipment rather than forge new tools.

11. *Lira*, 45 (1410), 90v.

12. *Lira*, 49 (1411), 235–35v.

13. *Lira*, 61 (1467), 162v.

14. See Mazzi and Raveggi, *Gli uomini*, 240.

15. See ibid., 73.

16. *Ricordanze di Oderigo di Andrea di Credi, orafo, cittadino fiorentino*, ed. F. Polidori, in *Archivio storico italiano* 4 (1843): 84.

17. G. Piccinni, *"Seminare, fruttare, raccogliere"* (Milan, 1982), 51; Mazzi and Raveggi, *Gli uomini*, 20. See also, in general, G. Duby, *The Early Growth of the European Economy: Warriors and Peasants from the Seventh to the Twelfth Century*, trans. H. Clarke (London, 1974), 53, and, on the area of Florence, G. Pinto, "L'Impruneta e Firenze: Contadini e proprietari, assetto delle colture e consumi," in *Impruneta, una pieve, un paese* (Florence, 1981) 30.

18. Mazzi and Raveggi, *Gli uomini*, 231; see also Pinto, "L'Impruneta," 23.

19. A 22v.

20. B 33v. Instead, we can deduce nothing from the gown that Benedetto bought for his niece Giovanna (B 16).

21. L. B. Alberti, *The Family in Renaissance Florence*, trans. R. Neu Watkins (Columbia, S.C., 1969), 194. G. Galasso, "Civiltà materiale e vita nobiliare in un inventario calabrese del '500," *Rivista storica italiana* 90 (1978): 747, notes that even in the better-off classes there

emerges "a visible contrast between domestic, interior, daily life, basically very sober, or even humble in dress, furniture, utensils, etc., and a social, public, exterior life marked by luxury, prestige, ostentation."

22. A 18.

23. See Mazzi and Raveggi, *Gli uomini*, 230–31.

24. Ibid., 209.

25. A 9–10.

26. B 7v. We know almost nothing about their linens. Only when a loan is repaid to the pawnbroker Francesco Petrocci do we find "one tablecloth eight arm's-lengths long, quite threadbare, five towels sewn together, six napkins sewn together" (A 20v). These reveal no more than the "clothes" bought for 36 lire by Pietro, Benedetto's son (A 21) about the real extent of the household linens. There is no reference to tools. Only once was the purchase of ropes, of unspecified cost, noted (B 3). There are no references to pots and kitchen utensils.

27. *Lira*, 72 (1479), 132.

28. *Lira*, 91 (1488), 111v; 103 (1493–95), 125v.

29. *Lira*, 106 (1498), 93v.

30. *Lira*, 111 (1509), 135. See A. K. Isaacs, "Popolo e Monti nella Siena del primo Cinquecento," *Rivista storica italiana* 82 (1970): 40, on the 50-lire limit.

31. *Lira*, 130 (1549), 84.

4. A Peasant Saga

1. See the *Lira*, 45 (1410), 90v; 49 (1411), 235.

2. See D. Herlihy and C. Klapisch-Zuber, *The Tuscans and Their Families: A Study of the Florentine Catasto of 1427* (New Haven, 1985), 301–2, 305, 472–76; E. Conti, *La formazione della struttura agraria* (Rome, 1966), vol. 1, 328, 333, 348, and vol. 3, 24, 36, 59, 76, 98, 108, 121, 144, 160, 176, 196, 294.

3. *Gabella contratti*, 195, March 1, 1438, 50.

4. *Gabella contratti*, 199, January 7, 1440; B 60–61.

5. *Gabella contratti*, 202, June 16, 1441, 8v.

6. *Gabella contratti*, 207, December 2, 1443, 7v.

7. *Gabella contratti*, 210, July 7, 1445, 7.

8. *Lira*, 158 (1465).

9. See G. Piccinni, *"Seminare, fruttare, raccogliere"* (Milan, 1982), 138.

10. *Lira*, 158 (1465).

11. *Gabella contratti*, 225, January 26, 1454, 25v.

12. B 13.

13. B 16.

14. B 53v.

15. *Gabella contratti*, 263, July 20, 1471, 20.

16. *Lira*, 181 (1478). L. A. Kotel'nikova, *Mondo contadino e città in Italia dall'XI al XIV secolo*

(Bologna, 1975), 41–51, discusses the preference for payments in kind in the late Middle Ages.

17. See A. Sapori, "I mutui dei mercanti fiorentini del Trecento e l'incremento della proprietà fondiaria," in *Studi di storia economica*, vol. 1 (Florence, 1955), 197.

18. *Gabella contratti*, 265, September 6, 1472, 35v.

19. *Lira*, 181 (1478),

20. *Gabella contratti*, 281, November 17, 1480, 13.

21. *Lira*, 204 (1483–84); 218 (1488).

22. *Lira*, 158 (1465).

23. Herlihy and Klapisch-Zuber, *Tuscans*, 210.

24. G. Morelli, *Ricordi*, ed. A. Schiaffini (Florence, 1969), 207–8.

25. D. Herlihy, "Marriage at Pistoia in the Fifteenth Century," *Bullettino storico pistoiese*, ser. 3, 7 (1972): 3–21; Herlihy and Klapisch-Zuber, *Tuscans*, 210–11.

26. Morelli, *Ricordi*, 212.

27. *Il libro segreto di Gregorio Dati*, ed. C. Gargiolli (Bologna, 1968), 31–32, 40–47, 74–79, 101–4.

28. See C. Klapisch-Zuber, "L'Enfance en Toscane au debut du XV siècle," *Annales de demographie historique* (1973): 9–122.

29. See G. Giorgetti, *Contadini e proprietari nell'Italia moderna* (Turin, 1974), 34.

30. *Lira*, 218 (1488).

31. *Lira*, 204 (1483–84).

32. On women's work, see Giorgetti, *Contadini e proprietari*, 34. Piccinni, "*Seminare*," 118, discusses spinning and weaving. G. Pinto, "Il personale, le balie e i salariati dell'ospedale di San Gallo di Firenze negli anni 1395–1406," *Ricerche storiche* 4 (1974): 128–32, and G. Cherubini, "Dal libro di ricordi di un notaio senese del Trecento," in his *Signori, contadini, borghesi* (Florence, 1974), 408–10, consider wet-nursing.

33. L. Sandri, *L'ospedale di S. Maria della Scala di S. Gimignano nel Quattrocento* (Florence, 1982), 128. See also Herlihy and Klapisch-Zuber, *Tuscans*, 234–41; and E. R. Coleman, "L'Infanticide dans le Haut Moyen Auge," *Annales E.S.C.* 29 (1974): 315–35.

34. See L. A. Kotel'nikova, "Le operazioni di credito e di usura nei secoli XI–XIV," *Rivista di storia dell'agricoltura* 13 (1973): 5; E. Cristiani, "Note sulla legislazione antiusuraia pisana," *Bollettino storico pisano*, ser. 3, 22–23 (1953–54): 13–15; P. Jones, "Forme e vicende di patrimoni privati nelle "Ricordanze" fiorentine del Trecento," in *Economia e società nell'Italia medievale* (Turin, 1980), 352; G. Pinto, "Aspetti dell'indebitamento e della crisi della proprietà," in his *La Toscana nel tardo Medioevo* (Florence, 1982), 208–9. There are interesting considerations, for a slightly later period in G. Corazzol, "Prestatori e contadini nella campagna feltrina intorno alla prima metà del '500," *Quaderni storici* 9 (1974): 450. For comparison with the Franche Conté in the 1500s, see L. Fèbvre, *Filippo II e la Franca contea* (Turin, 1979), 150–54.

35. *Lira*, 218 (1488).

36. *Lira*, 181 (1478).

37. *Lira*, 218 (1488).

38. *Lira*, 158 (1465).

39. *Lira*, 204 (1483–84); *Lira*, 218 (1488).
40. *Lira*, 110 (1498), 118v.
41. *Lira*, 451 (1497–1530), 1079v.
42. *Lira*, 111 (1509), 135.
43. *Gabella contratti*, 307, August 11, 1493, 15v.
44. *Gabella contratti*, 314, September 12, 1497, 62. Although we do not learn the size of this plot, we know Benedetto's share was one-quarter of the whole.
45. *Lira*, 369 (1528), 110.
46. *Lira*, 122 (1531), 204.
47. *Lira*, 181 (1478).
48. *Gabella contratti*, 227, December 29, 1454, 13.
49. Women who managed farmland appear seldom in late medieval Tuscany; see Herlihy and Klapisch-Zuber, *Tuscans*, 299.
50. Consider the case of cattle, whose loss of value was equally divided by the two brothers (A 14–14v).
51. *Lira*, 158 (1465) and *Gabella contratti*, 259, September 19, 1469, 40.
52. *Lira*, 181 (1478).
53. Sapori, "I mutui," 189–99.
54. *Lira*, 181 (1478).
55. B 58v.
56. *Lira*, 181 (1478). On Siena's Monte di Pietà, see N. Mengozzi, *Il Monte dei Paschi di Siena*, vol. 1 (Siena, 1891).
57. I. Capechhi and L. Gai, *Il Monte della Pietà a Pistoia* (Florence, 1975), 83–86; M. Ciardini, *I banchieri ebrei in Firenze nel secolo XV e il Monte di Pietà* (Florence, 1975), 80–81 and *Il Monte di Credito in Pegno di Pisa*, 91–94; D. Balestracci, "Lavoro e povertà in Toscana alla fine del Medioevo," *Studi storici* 23 (1982): 580.
58. C. De la Roncière, "Solidarités familiales et lignagères," in *Civiltà ed economia agricola* (Pistoia, 1981), 134.
59. C. Klapisch-Zuber, "'Parenti, amici e vicini,'" *Quaderni storici* 11 (1976): 957.
60. A 14–14v.
61. *Lira*, 158 (1465).
62. B 41v.
63. B 58v.
64. B 57v, 36.
65. B 43, 51–51v, 52–52v.

5. The Story of a Peasant

1. *Gabella contratti*, 195, April 25, 1438, c. 53.
2. B 35v.
3. A 5.
4. A 5v.

5. G. Pinto, "Ordinamento delle colture e proprietà fondiaria cittadina," in his *La Toscana nel tardo Medioevo* (Florence, 1982), 180; on "mixed" rent payments, see also G. Giorgetti, *Contadini e proprietari nell'Italia moderna* (Turin, 1974), 66–67.

6. On transportation, see L. A. Kotel'nikova, *Mondo contadino e città in Italia dall'XI al XIV secolo* (Bologna, 1975), 313. Benedetto's arrangements are in A 5v.

7 On demographics, see G. Cherubini, "Le campagne italiane dall'XI al XV secolo," in *Storia d'Italia*, vol. 4 (Turin, 1981), 433.

8. A 6v.

9. A 10v. See G. Giorgetti, *Contadini e proprietari nell'Italia moderna* (Turin, 1974), 144–45 and Kotel'nikova, *Mondo*, 312, on duration of contract.

10. See Giorgetti, *Contadini e proprietari*, 59, 63–64.

11. See A 4–12.

12. *Gabella contratti*, 225, January 26, 1453, c. 25v. See also *Lira*, 158 (1465).

13. B 6, 10.

14. *Lira*, 158 (1465).

15. Ibid.

16. *Gabella contratti* 199, January 7, 1440, c. 30; *Notarile*, 593, November 29, 1473, fasc. 90.

17. See G. Cherubini, "La proprietà fondiaria di un mercante toscano del Trecento," in his *Signori, contadini, borghesi*, 345–47, and S. Pivano, *Contratti agrari in Italia nell'alto medioevo* (Turin, 1904; rpt. Turin, 1969), 328.

18. *Gabella contratti*, 199, January 7, 1440, c. 30.

19. See Pivano, *Contratti*, 324; and B 60–60v.

20. *Lira*, 158 (1465).

21. *Notarile*, 593, November 25, 1473, fasc. 86.

22. The case is recorded fully in *Notarile*, 593, November 25 and 29, 1473, fasc. 86 and 90.

23. B 61.

24. *Gabella contratti*, 250, February 1, 1465, c. 18v.

25. See *Lira*, 61 (1467), c. 162v.

26. B 9.

27. *Gabella contratti*, 253, October 4, 1466, c. 46.

28. B 5.

29. See L. A. Kotel'nikova, "Condizione economica," in *Domanda e consumi, livelli e strutture*, ed. V. Barbagli Bagnoli (Florence, 1978), 94, 98; Giorgetti, *Contadini e proprietari*, 41–42; G. Cherubini, "Dal libro di ricordi di un notaio senese del Trecento," in his *Signori, contadini, borghesi* (Florence, 1974), 420. For information on landlords who paid off new sharecroppers' old debts, see G. Piccinni, "Seminare, fruttare, raccogliere" (Milan, 1982), 57–59. B. Machiavelli, *Libro di ricordi*, ed. C. Olschki (Florence, 1954), 3, wrote "I have to loan them [a sharecropper family entering his service] money for all of July, which is 30 lire to be paid to their former landlord Nicolo Doffi."

30. I. Imberciadori, *Mezzadria classica toscana* (Florence, 1951), 62, describes livestock-

sharing contracts; see also his "I due poderi di Bernardo Machiavelli, ovvero Mezzadria poderale nel'400," in *Studi in onore di Armando Sapori*, vol. 2 (Milan, 1957), 838 and D. Herlihy and C. Klapisch-Zuber, *The Tuscans and Their Families: A Study of the Florentine Catasto of 1427* (New Haven, 1985), 118-19.

31. The clauses are in B 10. See Giorgetti, *Contadini e proprietari*, 149; Cherubini, "Dal libro," 419; Piccinni, *"Seminare,"* 94-95, and Kotel'nikova, "Condizione economica," 95 and *Mondo*, 301.

32. B 11.

33. B 12.

34. *Gabella contratti*, 263, July 20, 1471, c. 20; *Lira*, 181 (1478).

35. See Giorgetti, *Contadini e proprietari*, 285. Elsewhere it was customary for landlords to furnish the animals (P. Jones, "From Manor," in *Florentine Studies*, ed. N. Rubinstein [London, 1968], 224; Kotel'nikova, "Condizione economica," 94). But indebtedness from the need to buy animals was common for sharecroppers (S. Tortoli, "Il podere e i mezzadri di Niccoluccio di Cecco della Boccia, mercante cortonese a Siena," *Ricerche storiche* 10 [1980]: 277; Herlihy and Klapisch-Zuber, *Tuscans*, 119), though peasants sometimes owned their own smaller animals.

36. The division of seed is "classic" in these contracts (Imberciadori, *Mezzadria*, 52). This custom spread in the late 1300s (Cherubini, "Dal libro," 419-20; Piccinni, *"Seminare,"* 54) and became subject to endless refinements in the 1400s (Imberciadori, "I due poderi," 838; Kotel'nikova, "Condizione economica," 94).

37. See Giorgetti, *Contadini e proprietari*, 39, for details on hay and manure divisions.

38. See Piccinni, *"Seminare,"* 92-93; Kotel'nikova, "Condizione economica," 95; Tortoli, "Il podere e i mezzadri," 271, for comparative data.

39. This was normal (Cherubini, "Dal libro," 419; Giorgetti, *Contadini e proprietari*, 45), but peasants tried to end the custom by which they had to transport produce to landowners' houses (Piccinni, *"Seminare,"* 88).

40. See Kotel'nikova, "Condizione economica," 94-95; Cherubini, "Le campagne italiane," 432; G. Pinto, "Forme di conduzione e rendita fondiaria nel contado fiorentino," in *La Toscana nel tardo Medioevo*, 295-96; and Piccinni, *"Seminare,"* 91-102, on the 1400s. Giorgetti, *Contadini e proprietari*, 43-48, describes the worsening conditions of the 1500s.

41. See P. Cammarosano, "Le campagne senesi dalla fine del secolo XII agli inizi del Trecento" in *Contadini e proprietari nella Toscana moderna*, vol. 1 (Florence, 1979), 200, 203, on the reasons smallholders and city folk entered into these agreements. Earlier it had been difficult to own and sharecrop lands at the same time: P. Cammarosano, *Le campagne nell'eta comunale* (Turin, 1974), 130-31.

42. Examples are in Herlihy and Klapisch-Zuber, *Tuscans*, 117-18; E. Conti, *La formazione della struttura agraria* (Rome, 1966), vol. 3, 12; M. S. Mazzi and S. Raveggi, *Gli uomini e le cose nelle campagne fiorentine del Quattrocento* (Florence, 1983), 86, 265; Jones, "From Manor," 236-37.

43. Giorgetti, *Contadini e proprietari*, 62.

44. See Imberciadori, *Mezzadria*, 68; M. Luzzati, "Toscana senza mezzadria," in *Contadini e proprietari nella Toscana moderna*, vol. 1 (Florence, 1979), 292.

45. Pinto, "Forme," 276–78, documents Florentine examples of renters becoming share-croppers, then renters again, after a natural catastrophe and recovery. Around 1400, peasants preferred sharecropping, which made payments easier in times of crisis (Jones, "From Manor," 226–27). I am not an apologist for sharecropping like some earlier historians, but do recognize that while sharecropping deprived peasants of ownership, the system could advance the material interests of peasants (see Cherubini, "La proprietà," 392 and again in *Civiltà ed economia agricola* (Pistoia, 1981), 166).

46. *Gabella contratti*, 274, June 8, 1476, c. 92.

47. *Notarile*, 656, October 30, 1479, fasc. 34; *Notarile*, 706, May 13, 1483, fasc. 71.

48. *Lira*, 200 (1481).

49. *Notarile*, 656, October 30, 1479, fasc. 34.

50. Ibid.; *Gabella contratti*, 279, October 30, 1479, c. 25v.

51. *Notarile*, 525, September 23, 1483.

52. B 23.

53. A 16; B 34, 37v, 44v-45.

54. B 27.

55. B 25v. Mattia was buried in the Magione church in Siena, which owned this land. See A. Sapori, "Case e botteghe a Firenze nel Trecento," in his *Studi di storia economica*, vol. 1, 309, on the use of November 1 to begin rent contracts.

56. On Aringhieri, see E. Carli, *Il Pintoricchio* (Milan, 1960), 66–67; F. Zeri, "Lo spettacolo intarsiato," *F.M.R.*, no. 6 (September 1982), 37–52.

57. B 41.

58. B 31v.

59. *Lira*, 200 (1481).

60. B 44.

61. *Notarile*, 525, September 23, 1483.

62. B 44.

63. L. Dominici, *Cronache*, ed. G. C. Gigliotti (Pistoia, 1933–39), vol. 2, 130; A. M. Nada Patrone, *L'ascesa della borghesia nell'Italia comunale* (Turin, 1974), 72.

64. A Sienese novelist of the 1400s who knew the countryside well, Gentile Sermini (*Novelle*, ed. G. Vettori (Rome, 1968), vol. 1, 149) advised, "if a controversy arises with the peasant, do not punish him with your own hands, but with the court." See B 50–50v. The payments are scattered throughout booklet B.

65. B 58.

66. B 43; *Lira*, 223 (1488); 213 (1483–84).

67. *Gabella contratti*, 285, June 11, 1482, c. 5v.

68. B 35; *Lira*, 213 (1483–84).

69. *Lira*, 223 (1488).

70. *Notarile*, 706, May 13, 1483, fasc. 71.

71. See A. Sapori, "L'usura nel Dugento a Pistoia," in his *Studi di storia economica*, vol. 1, 181–89. In the fourteenth century, permissible interest could reach 30 percent or even 40 percent in some Tuscan towns (A. Sapori, "L'interesse del denaro a Firenze nel Trecento,"

in his *Studi di storia economica*, vol. 1, 236). After 1400, 25 percent was considered licit, though 20 percent was normal (U. Cassuto, *Gli ebrei a Firenze nell'età del Rinascimento* (Florence, 1918; rpt. Florence, 1965),119–60).

72. We can reconstruct this operation from the resale of the land in *Gabella contratti* 295, August 7, 1487, c. 23.

73. Benedetto cheated the tax office on this occasion, declaring that the land had only vines (it also had arable) and was worth 70 fiorini (rather than 95) while his debt of 40 fiorini was declared as 45.

74. *Gabella contratti*, 290, November 25, 1484, c. 6v; B 46.

75. *Lira*, 223 (1488).

76. *Gabella contratti*, 305, October 30, 1492, c. 62.

6. The Women of the Household

1. He calls them "mezze maschie" in his *Prediche volgari* 4. R. Greci, "Donne e corporazioni," in A. Groppi, ed. *Il lavoro delle donne* (Bari, 1996), 71–91.

2. G. Piccinni, "Le donne nella vita economica, sociale e politica dell'Italia medievale," in A. Groppi, ed. *Il lavoro delle donne* (Bari, 1996), 5–46.

3. *Lira*, 158 (1465).

4. *Gabella contratti*, 195, April 25, 1438, c. 53.

5. B 1v, 4.

6. See A. Burguière, "Endogamia e comunità contadine," *Quaderni storici* 11 (1976): 1084.

7. E. Le Roy Ladurie, *The Peasants of Languedoc*, trans. J. Day (Urbana, Ill., 1974), 33, on customs regarding the management of dowries.

8. The Church considered ties between very remote relatives grounds for preventing marriage, even after the Fourth Lateran Council of 1215 relaxed strictures: J. L. Flandrin, *Amori contadini* (Milan, 1980), 15–21; R. Merzari, *Il paese stretto: Strategie matrimoniali nella diocesi di Como* (Turin, 1981), 11–22.

9. See C. De la Roncière, "Solidarités familiales et lignagères," in *Civiltà ed economia agricola* (Pistoia, 1981), 138; J. L. Flandrin, *La famiglia: Parentela, casa, sessualità nella società preindustriale* (Milan, 1979), 63–64; Burguière, "Endogamia," 1079–81.

10. D. Herlihy and C. Klapisch-Zuber, *The Tuscans and Their Families: A Study of the Florentine Catasto of 1427* (New Haven, 1985), 203.

11. B 52; *Gabella contratti*, 285, June 11, 1482, c. 5v. Lisabetta di Pietro's husband Girolamo (A 23v) came from an unspecified place.

12. De la Roncière, "Solidarités familiales et lignagères," 139, suggests from Valdelsa evidence that richer peasants sometimes married into urban families, whereas poorer ones always married rural people.

13. A 22v.

14. See M. S. Mazzi and S. Raveggi, *Gli uomini e le cose nelle campagne fiorentine del Quattrocento* (Florence, 1983), 105.

15. P. Cammarosano, "Aspetti delle strutture familiari nelle città dell'Italia comunale," in *Famiglia e parentela nell'Italia medievale*, ed. G. Duby and J. Le Goff (Bologna, 1981), 112.

16. Dowries are treated by N. Tamassia, *La familia italiana nei secoli decimoquinto e decimosesto*, (n.p., n.d.; rpt. Rome, 1971), 266–310; M. Bellomo, *Ricerche sui rapporti patrimoniali tra coniugi* (Milan, 1961) (with a fine bibliography); Cammarosano, "Aspetti"; and D. Owen Hughes, "Struttura famigliare e sistemi di successione ereditaria nei testamenti dell'Europa medievale," *Quaderni storici* 11 (1976), 934–40.

17. See G. Cherubini, "Il mondo contadino," in *Medioevo rurale*, ed. V. Criagelli and E. Rossetti (Bologna, 1980), 433; A. Sapori, "I mutui dei mercanti fiorentini del Trecento e l'incremento della proprietà fondiaria," in *Studi di storia economica*, vol. 1 (Florence, 1955), 192; G. Piccinni, *"Seminare, fruttare, raccogliere"* (Milan, 1982), 150, on how peasants assembled dowries.

18. *Consilio generale*, 236, February 10, 1476, c. 219.

19. *Gabella contratti*, 195, April 25, 1438, c. 53; *Gabella contratti*, 212, August 20, 1446, c. 25v.

20. *Gabella contratti*, 227, December 29, 1453, c. 13; *Gabella contratti*, 301, October 28, 1490, c. 71v.

21. *Gabella contratti*, 271, October 18, 1475, c. 65.

22. *Gabella contratti*, 251, August 14, 1465, c. 30.

23. A 23v alone shows Lisabetta's dowry to have included ten gold ducats in 1499.

24. B 63.

25. "Nunlike" (here translated as "hooded") refers to a dark-reddish colored cloth; see A 22v.

26. See Cammarosano, "Aspetti," 112, and J. Heers, *Family Clans in the Middle Ages*, trans. B. Herbert (Amsterdam, 1977), 211–12, on the custom of returning a dead woman's dowry to her biological family.

27. *Gabella contratti*, 285, June 11, 1482, c. 5v.

28. B 51–51v.

29. B 30v-31.

7. Cultivation and Animal Husbandry

1. On arboriculture, see S. Tortoli, "Il podere e i mezzadri di Niccoluccio di Cecco della Boccia, mercante cortonese a Siena," *Ricerche storiche* 10 (1980): 271–72; G. Pinto, "Ordinamento delle colture e proprietà fondiaria cittadina," in his *La Toscana nel tardo Medioevo* (Florence, 1982), 188–89; G. Cherubini, "Le campagne italiane dall'XI al XV secolo," in *Storia d'Italia*, vol. 4 (Turin, 1981), 378. For law, see *Constituto (II) del Comune di Siena dell'anno 1262*, ed. L. Zdekauer (Milan, 1897; rpt. Bologna, 1974), 283–84.

2. On the Tuscan fruit market, see C. De la Roncière, *Prix et salaires à Florence au XIV siècle*, (Aix-en-Provence, 1976), vol. 5, 211–22; Pinto, "Ordinamento," 193. As in earlier times, fruit was not eaten much (A. M. Nada Patrone, *Il cibo del ricco ed il cibo del povero* [Turin, 1981],

183; A. Cortonesi, "Le spese in victualibus della Domus Helemosine Sancti Petri di Roma," *Archeologia medievale* 8 [1981]: 208; C. Beck Bossard, "L'alimentazione in un villaggio siciliano del XIV secolo," *Archeologia medievale* 8 [1981]: 312; M. Montanari, *L'alimentazione contadina nell'alto Medioevo* [Naples, 1979], 368). The attention paid to fruit trees in agricultural treatises is noted by L. De Angelis, "I trattati di agricoltura," *Archeologia medievale* 8 (1981): 90, while Pinto, "Ordinamento," 192-95, analyzes sharecroppers' disdain for this type of agriculture.

3. See G. Duby, *Rural Economy and Country Life in the Medieval West*, trans. C. Postan (London, 1968), 65; urban markets resisted anything but wheat bread (G. Pinto, *Il libro del Biadaiolo* [Florence, 1978], passim; De la Roncière, *Prix*, 114-15), but peasants too preferred wheat bread (see G. Piccinni, *"Seminare, fruttare, raccogliere"* [Milan, 1982], 144-45).

4. G. Pinto, "Le colture cerealicole," in *La Toscana nel tardo Medioevo* (Florence, 1982), 113; Piccinni, *"Seminare,"* 146-49, on Siena; E. Conti, *La formazione della struttura agraria* (Rome, 1966), vol. 3, on Florence.

5. *Lira*, 158 (1465). Not even the suggestion of G. Giorgetti, *Le crete senesi nell'età moderna* (Turin, 1974), 88, allows accurate reconstructions here.

6. *Lira*, 181 (1478).

7. B 58v.

8. Unfortunately, there is only a single, vague reference to the Massarizias' cultivation of broad beans (*Notarile*, 706, May 13, 1483, fasc. 81), so we cannot know what role this fertilizing and nutricious crop had in the family's agriculture (it was very important in late medieval Tuscany: see Pinto, "Le colture," 104, 117, 125; Piccinni, *"Seminare,"* 35).

9. *Lira*, 218 (1488).

10. A 17.

11. In Tuscany it was not until the 1800s that crops of hay were grown. Earlier, tree leaves and shoots, especially in times of drought, were preferred (H. Desplanques, "Contribution a l'étude des paysages ruraux en Italie centrale," in *Geographie et histoire agraires* [Nancy, 1959], passim, and F. Sigaut, "Gli alberi da foraggio in Europa," *Quaderni storici* 17 [1982]: 50) although agricultural writers early advocated artificial meadows for fodder.

12. Uncultivated plots were sometimes reserved for peasants to farm in times of expanding agriculture (Tortoli, "Il podere e i mezzadri," 271-72).

13. See G. Pinto, "Le strutture ambientali e le basi dell'economia rurale," in his *La Toscana nel tardo Medioevo* (Florence, 1982), 36, on the "mixed" landscape of the hill areas.

14. On gardens, see Montanari, *L'alimentazione*, 314; E. Sereni, *History of the Italian Agricultural Landscape*, trans. R. Burr Litchfield (Princeton, 1997), 70; De Angelis, "I trattati," 88.

15. See Giorgetti, *Le crete*, 63.

16. From ancient times, thanks to their extensive root system, olives thrived in dry, hilly terrains (C. E. Stevens, "Agriculture and Rural Life in the Later Roman Empire," in *The Cambridge Economic History of Europe*, vol. 1, ed. M. Postan [Cambridge, 1966], 100). Olivoculture declined in the early Middle Ages (C. Bertagnolli, *Delle vicende dell'agricoltura in Italia* [Florence, 1977], 117-18), but oil production was not neglected everywhere (G. Pasquali, "Olivo e olio nell Lombardia prealpina," *Studi medievali*, ser. 3, 13 [1972]: 265).

17. *Notarile*, 706, May 13, 1483, fasc. 71; *Gabella contratti*, 295, August 7, 1487, c. 23.

18. See Stevens, "Agriculture," 100.

19. B 47v. On the ditches, whose bottom was covered with brambles and stones, in which olive trees were planted, see L. De Angelis, "Tecniche di coltura agraria e attrezzi agricoli alla fine del Medioevo," in *Civiltà ed economia agricola* (Pistoia, 1981), 211.

20. Following Pliny, late medieval and early modern agronomists advised this.

21. Although there was considerable trade in olive oil in Renaissance Tuscany (De la Roncière, *Prix*, 211–12, 540), this food was imported at least until the sixteenth century from areas of specialized production (F. Melis, "Note sulle vicende storiche dell'olio d'oliva," in *Dell'olio e della sua cultura* [Florence, 1972], 16–17). In Tuscany olive oil was less important and may have lost supremacy to animal fats during the Middle Ages, unlike what happened in Latium or farther south (C. Bertagnolli, *Delle vicende dell'agricoltura in Italia* [Florence, 1977], 118–19; J. L. Flandrin and O. Redon, "Les livres de cuisine italiens," *Archeologia medievale* 8 [1981]: 403–5; Pinto, "Ordinamento," 189; I. Ait, "Il commercio delle derrate alimentari nell Roma del'400," *Archeologia medievale* 8 [1981]: 166; Cortonesi, "Le spese," 210).

22. Pinto, "Ordinamento," 191–92, writes of peasant resistance to encroachment on "bread land" by trees whose first crop was years away. For comparative data from northern Italy, see A. I. Pini, "Due colture specialistiche del Medioevo," in *Medioevo rurale*, ed. V. Fumagalli and G. Rossetti (Bologna, 1981), 129–33; Pasquali, "Olivo e olio," 265.

23. B 49v.

24. See especially A. Marescalchi and G. Dalmesso, *Storia delle vite e del vino in Italia* (Milan, 1931–33); A. I. Pini, "La viticoltura italiana nel Medioevo," *Studi medievali*, ser. 3, 15 (1974): 795–884; I. Imberciadori, "Vite e vigna nell'alto Medio Evo," in *Agricoltura e mondo rurale in Occidente nell'alto Medioevo* (Spoleto, 1966), 307–342. On the wine market, see F. Melis, "Gli aspetti economici e mercantili dei prodotti dell'agricoltura e dei vini toscani in rapporto all loro commercio nel mondo," *Atti dell'Accademia Italiana della Cucina* 2 (1969): 19–48, and his "Il consumo del vino a Firenze nei decenni attorno al 1400," *Arti e mercature* 4, nos. 6–7 (1967): 11–21, and H. Zug Tucci, "Un aspetto trascurato del commercio medievale del vino," in *Studi in memoria di Federigo Melis*, vol. 3 (Naples, 1978), 311–48. Pini, "Due colture," 120, discusses the sacrality of vines and olive trees. On Tuscany, see C. De la Roncière, "Alimentation et ravitaillement à Florence au XIV siecle," *Archeologia medievale* 8 (1981): 184.

25. See De la Roncière, "Alimentation," 138; E. Fiumi, "Economia e vita privata dei fiorentini nelle rilevazioni statistiche di Giovanni Villani," in *Storia dell'economia italiana*, vol. 1, ed. C. M. Cipolla (Turin, 1959), 352; C. Falletti Fossati, *Costumi senesi della seconda metà del secolo XIV* (Siena, 1881), 23.

26. See De la Roncière, *Prix*, 131.

27. Custom left valley bottoms to vines growing on trees: Sereni, *History*, 95–97. See also Imberciadori, "Vite e vigna," 322; C. Parain, "The Evolution of Agrarian Technique," in *Cambridge Economic History of Europe*, vol. 1, ed. M. M. Postan (Cambridge, 1966), 131; G. Cherubini, "Proprietari, contadini e campagne senesi all'inizio del Trecento," in his *Signori, contadini, borghesi* (Florence, 1974), 263–69.

28. See P. Jones, "Medieval Agrarian Society in Its Prime: Italy," in *Cambridge Economic History of Europe*, vol. 1 (Cambridge, 1966), 371.

29. See Pinto, "Ordinamento," 180.

30. De Angelis, "I trattati," 89.

31. See F. Melis, "Il consumo del vino a Firenze nei decenni attorno al 1400," *Arti e mercature* 4, nos. 6–7 (1967): 7 and his "Produzione e commercio dei vini italiani," *Annales cisalpines d'histoire sociale* 3 (1972): 112; I. Imberciadori, "Proprietà terriera di Francesco Datini e parziaria mezzadrile nel'400," *Economia e storia* 5 (1978): 257, 263; Pinto, "Ordinamento," 179–80, 186.

32. See Imberciadori, "Vite e vigna," 321.

33. See Pinto, "Ordinamento," 171, 181–82.

34. See *Lira*, 158 (1465); *Gabella contratti*, 225, January 26, 1453, c. 25v; *Lira*, 204 (1483–84); *Notarile*, 706, May 13, 1483, fasc. 71; *Gabella contratti*, 253, October 4, 1466, c. 46; *Notarile*, 525, September 23, 1483; A 6v, 10v.

35. A 26.

36. Landlords often accepted the peasants' share of wine as a means of debt repayment: Pinto, "Ordinamento," 181; G. Cherubini, "Dal libro di ricordi di un notaio senese del Trecento," in his *Signori, contadini, borghesi* (Florence, 1974), 422–23; E. Conti, *I catasti agrari della Repubblica fiorentina e il catasto particellare toscano (secoli XIV–XIX)* (Rome, 1966), 48. See also Oderigo di Credi, *Ricordanze di Odergo di Andrea di Credi, orafo, cittadino fiorentino*, ed. F. Polidori, in *Archivio storico italiano* 4 (1843), 78, 85, 102.

37. A 27v.

38. *Lira*, 158 (1465); *Lira*, 200 (1481); B 39.

39. See C. Bec, "Le paysan dans la nouvelle toscane," in *Civiltà ed economia agricola* (Pistoia, 1981), 34. Although there were regional nuances, the need for grain and specialized crops limited the herding of large animals (D. Herlihy and C. Klapisch-Zuber, *The Tuscans and Their Families: A Study of the Florentine Catasto of 1427* [New Haven, 1985], 94–95). In the Maremma west of Siena, however, herding was the speciality; this region supplied the others with oxen (Pinto, "Le strutture ambientali," 64; Herlihy and Klapisch-Zuber, *Tuscans*, 120–21) or offered pasturage to transhumant herds. After 1350, Siena regulated transhumance (I. Imberciadori, "Il primo Statuto della Dogana dei Paschi Maremmani," in *Per la storia della società rurale* (Parma, 1971), 107–40; G. Pinto, "Le campagne e la 'crisi,'" in *Storia della società italiana*, vol. 7, pt. 2 [Milan, 1982], 132–33).

40. A 1; A 2v.

41. A 6, 3–3v.

42. See Cherubini, "Le campagne italiane," 298; Imberciadori, "I due poderi," 837–43. See also Piccinni, "Seminare," 62.

43. See C. Klapisch-Zuber, "Mezzadria e insediamenti rurali alla fine del Medioevo," in *Civiltà ed economia agricola*, 156, 162; G. Pinto, "La mezzadria delle origini," in his *Toscana nel tardo Medioevo* (Florence, 1982), 230; and Alberti, *De re aedificatoria* 1.5.

44. A 14.

45. B 23.

46. B 58. On Bernardino di ser Pietro's Marciano farm, however, Benedetto had to take his own animals.

47. See Piccinni, *"Seminare,"* 63; Tortoli, "Il podere e i mezzadri," 266.

48. A 1v, 3–3v, 8v.

49. A 16v, 19v.

50. This rough average was even exceeded (new animals every two to three years) on the lands of the Benedictine abbey of Monte Oliveto: Piccinni, *"Seminare,"* 71.

51. On *soccida* contracts, see I. Imberciadori, *Mezzadria classica toscana* (Florence, 1951), 62; C. Pecorella, *Contratti di allevamento del bestiame nella regione piacentina nel XIII secolo* (Milan, 1975), 105–24. Especially for peasants too poor to raise large animals, the supply of sufficient manure was a thorny problem in pre-modern times (Giorgetti, *Le crete*, 98–99 offers statistics; see also Pecorella, *Contratti*, 18 and G. Giorgetti, *Contadini e proprietari nell'Italia moderna* [Turin, 1974], 49–50, 147).

52. See P. Jones, "From Manor," in *Florentine Studies*, ed. N. Rubinstein (London, 1968), 224; Pecorella, *Contratti*, 18. Giorgetti, *Contadini e proprietari*, 285, analyzes the sixteenth-century process whereby landlords sought to take over the profits of keeping animals.

53. See Pecorella, *Contratti*, 29.

54. The fifteenth-century change obliging sharecroppers to own the animals was part of the worsening of conditions for this type of laborer: Piccinni, *"Seminare,"* 77.

55. A 8v.

56. Piccinni, *"Seminare,"* 75–76; Cherubini, "La proprietà," 374.

57. B 8.

58. See Piccinni, *"Seminare,"* 79. In the 1800s, three sheep were kept for every hectare cultivated (Giorgetti, *Le crete*, 74). Sheep meat's consumption is treated by G. Pasquali, "I problemi dell'approvvigionamento alimentare nell'ambito del sistema curtense," 113; De la Roncière, "Alimentation," 184; Cortonesi, "Le spese," 215; F. Leverotti, "Il consumo della carne a Massa all'inizio del XV secolo," 232–33; M. Biasiotti and P. Isetti, "L'alimentazione dall'osteologia animale in Liguria," 242–43; S. Frescura Nepoti, "Macellazione e consumo della carne a Bologna," 286; C. Tozzi, "L'alimentazione nella Maremma medievale," 300; C. Beck Bossard, "L'alimentazione in un villaggio siciliano del XIV secolo," 314, all in *Archeologia medievale* 8 (1981). On cheese, see M. S. Mazzi, "Note per una storia dell'alimentazione nell'Italia medievale," in *Studi di storia medievale e moderna per Ernesto Sestan*, vol. 1 (Florence, 1980), 91.

59. See Bec, "Le paysan," 34.

60. See M. Baruzzi and M. Montanari, *Porci e porcari nel Medioevo*, (Bologna, 1981), 72.

61. On *soccida* contracts for pigs, see Baruzzi and Montanari, *Porci e porcari*, 71; Piccinni, *"Seminare,"* 78–79. On part-time swineherding, see Montanari, *L'alimentazione*, 233; Baruzzi and Montanari, *Porci e porcari*, 33.

62. Baruzzi and Montanari, *Porci e porcari*, 37.

63. See Baruzzi and Montanari, *Porci e porcari*, 73; Montanari, *L'alimentazione*, 233, 235,

241–44; and E. Faccioli, ed., *L'eccellenza e il trionfo del porco* (Milan, 1982), 165. See also F. Stouff, *Ravitaillement et alimentation en Provence* (Paris, 1970), 155; Baruzzi and Montanari, *Porci e porcari*, 67–69 on pig-slaughtering cooperatives.

64. B 10. On chickens, see De Angelis, "Tecniche," 208; Montanari, *L'alimentazione*, 250–53; Piccinni, *"Seminare,"* 78.

65. B 8–8v.

66. M. S. Mazzi and S. Raveggi, *Gli uomini e le cose nelle campagne fiorentine del Quattrocento* (Florence, 1983), 194–95.

67. B 21.

68. B 55v–56v.

69. See Duby, *Rural Economy*, 148.

70. A 3, 16v, B 15.

8. The Lime Kiln

1. G. Cherubini, "Le campagne italiane dall'XI al XV secolo," in *Storia d'Italia*, vol. 4 (Turin, 1981), 34.

2. Ibid., 309. The attack on the woodlands continued, with fluctuations, throughout Europe, climaxing in the sixteenth century (see C. M. Cipolla, *Before the Industrial Revolution: European Society and Economy, 1000–1700* [New York, 1980], 111–12; E. Sereni, *History of the Italian Agricultural Landscape*, trans. R. Burr [Princeton, 1997], 110; R. Romano, *Tra due crisi* [Turin, 1971], 58).

3. B 12v.

4. W. M. Bowsky, *The Finance of the Commune of Siena, 1287–1355* (Oxford, 1970), 133.

5. B 10.

6. Archivio di Stato di Siena, "Arti," 47: "Statuto dell'arte della Pietra," 1441, 8v.

7. See D. Balestracci and G. Piccinni, *Siena nel Trecento* (Florence, 1977), 24; L. Bortolotti, *Siena* (Bari, 1983), 57. For comparisons with Florence, see G. Pinto, "I livelli di vita dei salariati cittadini nel periodo successivo al tumulto dei ciompi," in *Il tumulto dei ciompi* (Florence, 1981), 174–76; and R. Goldthwaite, *The Building of Renaissance Florence* (Baltimore, 1980).

8. Even this "simple" kiln required the repairs of a specialist: in 1461 Benedetto paid one for fixing his kiln (B 4).

9. Vannoccio Biringuccio, *De la Pirotechnia* (Venice, 1540; rpt., ed. A. Carugo, Milan, 1977), 9, 146v.

10. See M. S. Mazzi and S. Raveggi, *Gli uomini e le cose nelle campagne fiorentine del Quattrocento* (Florence, 1983), 148, 267 for other examples of this.

11. B 20.

12. Thanks to Gabriella Piccinni, who found the record (*Patrimonio resti* 913, 1498, cc. 4, 29–30), we know that this deal provided Pietro and company with more than 22 lire and 21 soldi.

13. B 33.
14. B 40v.
15. B 1, 4.
16. A 9.
17. A 10.
18. D. Balestracci, "Introduzione" in *Statuto dell'Arte dei Muratori* (Siena, 1976), xvii;
V. Lusini, "Dell'arte del legname innanzi al suo statuto del 1426," *Bullettino senese di storia patria* 10 (1904): 183–246; *Breve dell'Arte de'maestri di Pietre senesi*, ed. G. Milanesi in *Documenti per la storia dell'arte senese*, vol. 1 (Siena, 1854), 105–35.
19. Compare the donations of a rich Florentine peasant (Mazzi and Raveggi, *Gli uomini*, 271) and the enthusiasm of peasants of the abbey of Monte Oliveto for the Bianchi penitents and for willing goods to the poor (G. Piccinni, "Seminare, fruttare, raccogliere" [Milan, 1982], 151–56).

9. A Family Confronts the State

1. J. Delumeau, *La Peur en Occident* (Paris, 1978), 167–70.
2. G. Cherubini, "Le campagne italiane dall'XI al XV secolo," in *Storia d'Italia*, vol. 4 (Turin, 1981), 431.
3. See P. Cammarosano, *Monteriggioni: Storia, architettura, paesaggio* (Milan, 1983), 77; and G. Piccinni, "I 'villani incittadinati' nella Siena del XIV secolo," *Bullettino senese di storia patria* 82–83 (1975–76): 186–203, on Siena's countryside in the 1300s.
4. W. M. Bowsky, *The Finance of the Commune of Siena, 1287–1355* (Oxford, 1970), 168–69; A. K. Isaacs, "Le campagne senesi fra Quattro e Cinquecento," in *Contadini e proprietari nella Toscana moderna*, vol. 1 (Florence, 1979), 381–82.
5. B 1.
6. A 4.
7. See Bowsky, *Finance*, 166–88 on forced loans.
8. Ibid., 171.
9. Ibid., 178. Similar interest rates prevailed at Venice (G. Luzzatto, *Il debito pubblico della repubblica di Venezia* [Milan, 1963], 36–37), Pisa (C. Violante, "Imposte dirette e debito pubblico nel basso Medioevo," in *Economia, società, istituzioni a Pisa nel Medioevo* [Bari, 1980], 122), and Florence (B. Barbadoro, *Le finanze della Repubblica fiorentina* [Florence, 1929]).
10. Violante, "Imposte," 122.
11. Bowsky, *Finance*, 187.
12. Compare Venice (Luzzatto, *Il debito*, 137–38).
13. Siena imposed very many loans in late 1200s and early 1300s (Bowsky, *Finance*, 186). In Venice a similar frequency after the war of Chioggia caused reactions (Luzzatto, *Il debito*, 106–7). These "exceptional" loans tended to become routine taxes (e.g., at Pisa: Violante, "Imposte," 118, 120, 121, 125, 126).

14. V. Buonsignori, *Storia della Repubblica di Siena,* vol. 2 (Siena 1856; rpt. Bologna, 1972), 42–44.
15. A 6v, 89.
16. A 7.
17. O. Malavolti, *Dell'historia di Siena* (Venice, 1599; rpt. Bologna, 1968), pt. 3, bk. 4, 74v.
18. *Lira,* 342 (1488) c. 110v.
19. *Lira,* 345 (1495) c. 12.
20. Malavolti, *Dell'historia di Siena,* pt. 3, bk. 6, 99–99v.
21. *Lira,* 451 (1497–1530) c. 1079–1079v; 358 (1500–2) cc. 162, 482.
22. *Lira,* 453 (1498) c. 847.
23. *Lira,* 354 (1500) c. 120v; 356 (1500) c. 103; 357 (1500) c. 71v; 363 (1502) c. 102v; 366 (1502–9) cc. 118, 119; 367 (1509) c. 136; 368 (1526) c. 94; 369 (1528) c. 110; 371 (1528) c. 93.

10. Exit from History

1. *Lira,* 158 (1465).
2. *Lira,* 200 (1481); 213 (1483–84); 223 (1488).
3. *Lira,* 223 (1488).
4. A 16; B 28v, 42v.
5. *Gabella contratti,* 251, August 14, 1465, c. 30.
6. B 23.
7. A 24–24v, 25–25v, 26–26v; B 20v-21, 40, 44v-45.
8. *Lira,* 181 (1478).
9. R. Merzari, *Il paese stretto: Strategie matrimoniali nella diocesi di Como,* (Turin, 1981), 63 notes the connection between excessive prolificity and economic ruin. A. K. Isaacs, "Le campagne senesi fra Quattro e Cinquecento," in *Contadini e proprietari nella Toscana moderna,* vol. 1 (Florence, 1979), 389–90, comments on fragmentation of holdings due to inheritance practices (see also D. Herlihy and C. Klapisch-Zuber, *The Tuscans and Their Families: A Study of the Florentine Catasto of 1427* [New Haven, 1985], 305). M. S. Mazzi and S. Raveggi, *Gli uomini e le cose nelle campagne fiorentine del Quattrocento* (Florence, 1983), 95 point out that smallholders were more vulnerable than others in this respect because they actually owned something.
10. A similar trend is observable in a declining urban family. As the Corsini of Florence grew poorer, they lost familiarity with writing and grammar (A. Petrucci, "Per la storia dell'alfabetismo e della cultura scritta: Metodi-materiali-quesiti," in *Alfabetismo e cultura scritta,* 39).
11. I found nothing in the carefully scoured court records of Siena's Archivio di Stato, though I even searched through the papers of ser Prospero di Niccolo di Battista, who recorded this incident, which he witnessed (*Lira,* 365, 1539, c. 139).
12. *Balia,* 964; *Bocche,* unnumbered pages.

Index

Page numbers in *italics* refer to illustrations.

account books
  agricultural diaries as, xviii–xix
  appearance of, 7–8, 9
  contracts and, 5
  family affairs in, 6
  general content of, x, 6–7
  handwriting in, 8
  origin of practice of, 1–2
  research on, 116 n. 6
  of subaltern classes, x, 2
  vernacular in, 9
acquarello (watery wine), 74
Agnolo, Girolamo d', 69
Agostoli, 18
agriculture, ix–x
  family help with, xii, 15, 38, 56
  historians' interest in, xviii, xix–xx
  intercultivation, 71
  in Masse, 11–12, 14–15, 18
  monoculture, 14
  tasks of, xi–xii
  women in, xii, 15, 39, 65
  See also sharecropping
Alberti, Leon Battista, 31, 77
Amadori, Astorre Andrea degli, 9
animals
  contracts and, 79–80
  debt for, 128 n. 35
  diet of, 72–73
  housing of, 77

  landowners' ownership of, 77–78, 79
  oxen, 134 n. 39
  pasturage of, 76–77
  pigs, 80–81
  sharecroppers' ownership of, 79–80,
    128 n. 35, 135 n. 54
  taxes and, 76
  turnover of, 135 n. 50
Archive of the Society of the Executors
  of Pious Dispositions, x
Aringhieri, Alberto, 8, 23, 56–57, 58
arrears payments, 57–58
Arte della Pietra, 85
attorneys, 48–49, 50. *See also* court
  matters

baccalari (know-it-alls), 5
Bartolomeo, Antonio di ser, 79
Bauml, F. H., 118 n. 12
beds, 31, 87–88
Belcaro, 18
Benucci, Francesco di Bartolomeo, 24,
  51, 77
Besso, Bernardino di Pietro di Nanni
  del, 53
Besso, Giacomo del, 77
Biccherna, xxiv
Bicci, Neri di, 2
Biringuccio, Vannoccio, 86
birthrates, 38

Index

Black Death, 17, 19, 46–47
Borghesi, Giacomo di Mariano, mortgages and, 41–42
Borghesi, Onofrio, 52
Borghesi, Tommaso di Mariano, land sales by, 36–37, 51, 52–53
Borghesi family, 24
bourgeoisie, village, 25–26, 29, 30
bread, 53, 72, 132 n. 3
broad beans, 132 n. 8
brooms, 73
burials, 6, 66, 129 n. 55

Camollia, 20
canna, definition of, xxiii
Carrara, Andrea da, 2
Casciano, 12, 33, 41, 47–48, 50–51, 73
Castelfranco di Sopra, 4
Catholic Church, 93, 130 n. 8. *See also* monasteries
Certano, 18
Cesario, Antonio di, 87
Cesario, Giovanni di, 77, 87
The Cheese and the Worms (Ginzburg), 4
Chele, Mariana di. *See* Massarizia, Mariana (Benedetto's wife)
Cherubini, Giovanni, xvii
chickens, 81
children
  agricultural roles of, xii, 15, 38
  mortality rate of, 38
  wet nurses and, 65–66
citizenship, in Siena, 19
Clanchy, M. T., 118 n. 12
class differences, 25–26, 29, 30, 123 n. 2. *See also* peasants
clothing, purchases of, 29, 31, 123 n. 20
commons, 14–15
communes, 18, 19
contracts, 4–5
  account books and, 5

landowners and (*see* landowners: contracts and)
literacy and, 119–20 n. 25
for marriages, 67–68 (*see also* dowries)
mezzadria (*see* sharecropping)
multiple, 17
rent (*see* rent contracts)
shelter, 54, 56
taxes on, 93
usufructuary, 34, 48
See also court matters
Corsini, Matteo di Niccolò, 38
countryside
  definition of, 3
  versus urban center, 23–25
  See also literacy: rural countryside and
court matters, 48–49, 50, 57–58, 91. *See also* contracts
Credi, Oderigo di Andrea di, 5, 29

Dati, Agostino, 41
Dati, Goro di Stagio, 38
Datini, Margherita, 65
debts
  for animals, 128 n. 35
  arrears payments, 57–58
  for dowries, 38–39
  for grain, 27, 37, 39, 42, 43, 53, 72, 94
  for land, 41–42
  landlords and, 127 n. 29
  long-term, 31, 55–57
  pawnbrokers and, 26, 42, 97
  payments in lime, 57, 87
  payments in wine, 46, 75–76, 134 n. 36
  for sharecropping, 52, 92
  for wood sales, 84
denari, definition of, xxii
depopulation, 19–20, 46–47, 54, 67–68
diet
  of animals, 72–73

Index

bread in, 53, 72, 132 n. 3
broad beans in, 132 n. 8
fruit in, 131 n. 2
olive oil in, 73–74
pork in, 80–81
poultry in, 81
wine in, 74
See also food
Dino, Giovanni, debts of, 60
Dino, Ser Giusto di ser, 55, 59
Dino, Vittorio, 60
Doffi, Nicolo, 127 n. 29
dowries, for marriages, xiii
amounts of, 26, 69
burden of, 63–64, 68–69
composition of, 29, 69
disputes over, 69–70, 98–99
indebtedness and, 38–39
land sales for, 43
records of, 7
reimbursements of, 58, 70
drainage canals, 53

education. *See* schools
The Effects of Good Government (painting)
(Lorenzetti), 12, *16*, 83, *84*
Esecutori di Gabella, xxiv

fallow lands, 73, 132 n. 12
family affairs, in account books, 6
famine, rent contracts in, 16
farming. *See* agriculture
feast days, 31
Feria, Bernardino di Antonio del, 25–26
Feria, Giovanni di Antonio del, 21,
25–26
Finetti, Memmo di Mariano, 24
firewood, 72
Florence
conflicts with Siena, 20
taxes in, 90

florin, definition of, xxii
food
purchases of, 25, 123 n. 8
sharecropping and, 18
See also diet
Fornicchia, 18
foundlings, 39, 64
fruit trees, 71–72

Gabella (registry office), xix
assessment of Massarizia family
wealth, 27, 28, 30
definition of, xxiv
land confiscations by, 6–7, 43
See also taxes
gabelle, definition of, xxiv
gardens, 73
Giacomo, Pasquino di, 9
Gino, Frusino di Donato di, 5
Ginzburg, Carlo, xviii, 4
grain, debt for, 27, 37, 39, 42, 43, 53,
72, 94
Guglielmo, Francesco di Bartolomeo di,
51–52
Guidino, Cristofano di, 42
guilds
masons, 85, 88
stoneworkers, 88
women in, 64

handwriting, in account books, 8
hay, 132 n. 11
herding, 134 n. 39
historians
interest in agriculture, xviii, xix–xx
on sharecropping, xi
horses, 81

illiteracy
agricultural diaries and, xviii–xix
definition of, 2–3, 8

141

Index

social impact of, xiv
See also literacy
infanticide, 39
installment payments
  for animals, 81
  for beds, 31
  for land, 51, 52, 55–56, 59–60, 61
insults, for peasants, 5
intercultivation, 71
interest
  cost of, 60
  on forced loans, 93, 95
  rates of, 129 n. 71, 137 n. 9
  versus rent, 55

landowners
  animals of, 77–78, 79
  contracts and, 4–5, 15, 36, 46, 48–
    50, 75
  as moneylenders, 42, 52, 127 n. 29
  obligations in sharecropping (*see* share-
    cropping: landowner obligations in)
  payments to, 134 n. 36
land sales and acquisitions, xii–xiii,
  14, 15
  confiscations and, 6–7, 43
  inheritance and, 138 n. 9
  of smallholders, 26, 34, 36–37,
    138 n. 9
  taxes on, 93
  See also Massarizia, Benedetto del: land
    sales and acquisitions of; Massarizia,
    Galgano: land sales and acquisitions
    of; Massarizia, Giovanni: land sales
    and acquisitions of; Massarizia,
    Meo: land sales and acquisitions of
Langeli, A. Bartoli, 116 n. 8, 117 n. 7
Lapini, Paolo di Giovanni, 68, 69
Latin, use of, 9
Lecceto, convent of, 12, 34, 42, 48–50
Leonardo, Giacomo di, 40

lime production, 72, 85–88
  in debt payment, 57, 87
  kilns and, 136 n. 8
  taxes on, 86, 92
  wood for, 136 n. 2
lira
  as basis for taxable wealth, xxiii–xxiv
  definition of, xxii
literacy, xiv
  contracts and, 119–20 n. 25
  peasants' use of, 5, 120 n. 29
  rural countryside and, xx–xxi, 2–3,
    116 n. 8, 117 n. 7, 118 nn. 8 and 12
  social impact of, xiii
  subsidization of education and, 3–4
  urbanism and, 138 n. 10
  See also illiteracy
livestock, purchases of, 81
loans
  forced, 19, 43, 93–94, 95, 137 n. 13
  from landlords, 42
  for taxes, 92–93, 137 n. 13
  war and forced, 94–95
Lopez, R. S., 118 n. 12
Lorenzetti, Ambrogio, 12, *16*, 83
luxury goods, 29, 31, 124 nn. 21 and 26

manure, 135 n. 50
Marciano, 12, 18, 47, 51, 55, 59
marriage brokers, 68
marriages
  age at, 33, 37–38
  arrangement of, xii, 66–67, 130 n. 12
  of Benedetto del Massarizia, 45–
    46, 66
  Catholic Church on, 130 n. 8
  contracts for, 67–68
  dowries for (*see* dowries, for marriage)
  effect of depopulation on, 67–68
  of Galgano del Massarizia, 66–67
Martini, Francesco di Giorgio, 12, *13*

Index

Martino, Gaspare di, 41, 42
Massaio, Brandina, 40
Massaio, Simonetto di, 5
Massarizia, Antonio, 39, 40
Massarizia, Benedetto del
    agricultural tasks of, xi–xii
    background of, x–xi
    business interests with brothers, 41,
        42–43
    debts of, 92
    decline in wealth of, 31–32
    donation of building material to
        churches, 88
    heirs of, 97–99
    land acquisitions and sales of, 36–
        37, 47, 50–51, 52–53, 59, 60–61,
        126 n. 44
    lime production of, 85–88
    marriages of, 45–46, 66
    reason for agricultural diaries of,
        xiv–xv
    as sharecropper, 48–50, 53, 56, 58
    sons of, 56, 77
    taxes of, 27, 29
    use of notaries by, 5, 8–9, 24, 70
    as village bourgeoisie, 25
    vineyards of, 75–76
    wine sales of, 76
    wood sales of, 85
Massarizia, Bernardina del, 68, 69
Massarizia, Bernardo del, 39–40
Massarizia, Betto del, 33
Massarizia, Cristofana del, xiii, 37–38,
    66–67, 69
Massarizia, Francesco del, 56
Massarizia, Galgano del, xiii, 7, 40
    death of, 58
    debts of, 43, 92
    heirs of, 97–99
    land acquisitions and sales of, 47, 58
    marriage of, 66–67

mortgages of, 41–42
    as sharecropper, 41
Massarizia, Giovanna del, xii
Massarizia, Giovanna del (Benedetto's
    wife), debts of, 7, 46
Massarizia, Giovanna del (Galgano's
    wife)
    dowry return to, 59
    marriage contract of, 67–68
Massarizia, Giovanni del, xiii, 7, 24, 26
    business interests of, 36
    heirs of, 97–99
    land acquisitions and sales of, 36–37,
        47, 52
    as rent landlord, 36
    as sharecropper, 34
    tax returns of, 37
Massarizia, Iacoma del, 69
Massarizia, Lorenzo del, 56, 77
Massarizia, Mariana del, xii, 6, 45, 66
Massarizia, Mattia del, 6, 56, 129 n. 55
Massarizia, Meo del, 7
    land sales and acquisitions of, xii–xiii,
        14, 15, 34, 40
    relocation to Casciano, 33
    relocation to Montalbuccio, 34
    role in family marriages, 66–67
    as sharecropper, 48
    taxes of, 27
    use of notaries by, 5
    wealth of, 39
Massarizia, Nanni del, 33, 34
    land sales and acquisitions of, xii–xiii
    taxes of, 27
Massarizia, Pietro del, 81
Massarizia, Ugolino del, 33
Massarizia, Vangelista del
    delayed dowry payments of, 67–68
    dowry dispute of, 69–70
    dowry of, 43
    land sales and acquisitions of, 58

Index

Massarizia family tree, diagram of, *35*
Masse region
  abandonment of, 19–20 (*see also*
    depopulation)
  agriculture in (*see* agriculture)
  descriptions of, 14, 120 n. 1
  map of, *xxv*
  Siena and, 12, *13* (*see also* Siena)
  See also sharecropping
meadows, 72–73
measurements, conversion to modern
  units, xxiii–xxiv
mercantile class
  influence of, 1–2, 7
  sharecropping origins and, 17
mercenary bands, 20
mezzadria. See sharecropping
moggio, definition of, xxiii
Momigliano, Arnaldo, xvii
monasteries
  Lecceto, 12, 34, 42, 48–50
  in Masse, 14
  Monte Oliveto abbey, 135 n. 50
  Ognissanti, 81
  San Galgano Abbey, 46
  San Martino, 92
  Sant' Agostino, 34
  taxes and, 122 n. 26
moneylenders, landlords as, 42, 52,
  127 n. 29
monoculture, 14
Montalbuccio, 12, 14
Monte di Pietà, 42, 97
Monte Oliveto abbey, 135 n. 50
Morelli, Giovanni di Pagolo, 38
mortgages, 41–42, 55–56, 60
mules, 81

notaries
  booklets provided by, 7–8
  Massarizia use of, 5, 8–9, 24, 70

role of, xiv–xv
writings of, 4–5

Ognissanti, convent of, 81
olive oil, 73–74, 132 n. 16, 133 n. 21
olive trees, 71–72, 73, 133 n. 22
oral culture versus written culture, 3, 4,
  119 n. 25. *See also* literacy
oxen, 76–77, 79–80, 134 n. 39

Pace, Paolo di, 6, 7
Palio festival, 93
Passara, Giorgio del, 26, 42
Passara, Leonardo del, 26
pasturage
  land for, 76, 77
  rights, 14–15, 78–79
pawnbrokers, role of, 26, 42, 97
payment in kind, 31, 87–88
Pazzi Conspiracy, 20–21
peasants
  account books of, x, 2
  buying habits of, 29
  contracts and (*see* contracts)
  education of, 3–4
  family solidarity of, 42–43
  fear of war, 25, 122 n. 29
  insults for, 5
  literacy and, 5, 120 n. 29
  marriage age of, 33, 37–38
  status concerns of, 29, 31
  stereotypes of, xx–xxi
  surnames of, 24
  testimonies of, 115 n. 5
  urban influences on, 24–25
  See also sharecropping: peasant obliga-
    tions in; subaltern class
Petroccio, Francesco, 23
Piccolomini, Aeneas Silvius, 14
pigs, 80–81
Pius II, Pope, 14

Index

polyculture, 14–15
priests, as teachers, 4
Provveditori, xxiv
purchasing power, calculation of, xxii–xxiii

Quercetano, 18

rent contracts, 16
versus interest, 55
landlords and, 36, 46, 75
versus sharecropping, 17, 129 n. 45
Roncière, C. de la, 116 n. 7

S. Maria al Monte, 3–4
salaries
for public officials, 90
for workers, xxiii
San Galgano Abbey, 46
San Martino, convent of, 92
San Martino, district of, 20
Sant' Agostino, convent of, 34
Santa Maria della Scala, xxii
schools
origins of, 3–4
subsidization of, 3–4, 118 n. 15,
119 n. 16
Sciascia, Leonardo, x
Scott, James C., xiv
Sega, Lippo di Fede del, 116 n. 7
Sermini, Gentile, 129 n. 64
sharecropping, 25–26
animals and, 79–80, 128 n. 35,
135 n. 54
debts for, 52, 92
decline of, 18
duration of, 15–16
effect of Black Death on, 46–47
food self-sufficiency in, 18
function of, xi, 17–18
historians on, xi

as income insurance, xi, 54–55, 56, 58
landowner obligations in, 15, 46–47,
53, 56, 58, 77–78, 79, 92
origins of, 15, 17
peasant obligations in, 15–16, 41, 46–
47, 52, 53, 78–79
versus rent contracts, 17, 129 n. 45
stereotypes of, xxi, 91–92
taxes and, 91–92
war and, 122 n. 29
womens' obligations in, 65
See also agriculture; contracts
sheep, 72–73, 80
shelter contracts, 54, 56
Siena
communes' relationship to, 19
conflicts with Florence, 20
Masse region and, 12, 13
taxes in, 19–20, 90, 91
soccida, 77–80
soldo, definition of, xxii
soma, definition of, xxiii
staioro, definition of, xxiii
status, peasant concern with, 29, 31
stereotypes
of peasants, xx–xxi
of sharecropping, xxi, 91–92
Strozzi, Alessandra Mancighi, 65
subaltern class
account books kept by, x, 2
cultural forms associated with, xvii
definition of, xiii
urban, xvii–xviii
See also peasants
surnames, in tax returns, 24

taverns, 4
taxes
amounts paid by individuals, 90
animals and, 76
burden on villages, 89–90

Index

cheating on, 37, 130 n. 73
on contracts, 93
dowries and, 63–64
in Florence, 90
forced loans as, 92–93, 137 n. 13
indirect, 92
on land sales and acquisitions, 93
on lime production, 86, 92
lira as basis for taxable wealth, xxiii–xxiv
Massarizia family, 27, 28, 29, 30, 37
monasteries and, 122 n. 26
number of taxpayers and, 122 n. 26
ordinary, 93
payments of, 26
on sharecroppers, 91–92
in Siena, 19–20, 90, 91, 137 n. 13
surname usage in, 24
on wood gathering, 92
See also Gabella (registry office)
teachers, subsidization of rural, 3–4, 118 n. 15, 119 n. 16
Terrenzano, 18, 60–61
textiles, 31, 124 n. 26
tithes, 93
tolls, xxiv, 53–54, 84, 128 n. 39
trees
    fruit, 71–72
    olive, 71–72, 73, 133 n. 22

Ugolino, Giovanni d', 9
Umidi, Antonio di Sano, 88
urbanocentrism, xvii–xviii, 4–5, 23–25, 91–92, 118 n. 12
usufructuary contracts, 34, 48

Vanni, Angelino di, 58
Vannocchia, Antonio di Vannucchio del, 27

Vannocchia, Pietro di Vannucchio del, 27
vernacular, in account books, 9
villages, structure of, 18, 19
vineyards, 74–76, 133 n. 27. *See also* wine
The Virgin Protecting Siena (painting) (Martini), *13*
Vitale, Bartolomeo di, 80
viticulture, 74–75. *See also* wine

war
    effects of, 20–21, 55, 94
    forced loans and, 94–95
    peasants' fear of, 25, 122 n. 29
    rent contracts in, 16
wet nurses, 65–66
"widened family, 15
wine, 46, 74, 75–76, 92, 134 n. 36
women
    agricultural roles of, xii, 15, 39, 65
    childbirth and, 38
    as economic burden, 26
    as farm managers, 126 n. 49
    in guilds, 64
    inheritance and, 65
    property and, 65
    as wet nurses, 65–66
wood
    cutting rights for, 84
    firewood, 72
    for lime production, 136 n. 2
    taxes on gathering, 92
    tolls and sales of, 84
woodland, 72
woolworkers, 68